Who Is God?

by

Harold R. Eberle

Worldcast Publishing
Yakima, Washington
United States

Who Is God?
© 2008 by Harold R. Eberle

Worldcast Publishing
P.O. Box 10653
Yakima, WA 98909-1653
United States of America
(509) 248-5837
www.worldcastpublishing.com
office@worldcastpublishing.com

Softbound ISBN: 978-1-882523-27-6
Hardbound ISBN: 978-1-882523-34-4
Cover by Paul Jones
Cover Photo by Michael Wade

Unless otherwise stated, Scriptures are taken from the New American Standard Bible, Copyright © 1960, 1962, 1963, 1968, 1971, 1972, 1973, 1975, 1977, 1995 by The Lockman Foundation.

Credits and Thanks

Who is God? In my search for an answer to this question I drew on numerous Bible teachers, pastors, and friends who helped me think through the issues, and in the process, added their insights and comments to this work. These include Pastor Odeworitse Eyeoyibo, Pastor John Garfield, Pastor John Klein, Dr. Daniel Juster, Joshua Eberle, Andrew Sievright, Pastor Bruce Latshaw, Pastor Bob Hall, Pastor Martin Trench, Peter Iseman, Rev. Keith Gerner, Pastor Jeff Berry, John Alcomo, Pastor Tom Verdam, and Pastor Pat McClusky. I also received seeds of inspiration from Dr. Clark Pinnock, Dr. C. Peter Wagner, and Pastor Ted Hansen. Even though I received so much wonderful help, none of these people should be held responsible for any ideas or mistakes herein.

James Bryson is my writing coach and more than anyone else, he contributed to this work. Sherrie St Hillaire added a touch of class and Annette Bradley is my grammar expert. I am blessed to have Tristan Kohl as my final editor, but I consider no book complete until my wife, Linda, has placed upon it her stamp of approval. Thanks to all of you.

Table of Contents

Foreword

Who is God?
The question echoes through the ages. Mystics seek him through blind eyes. Jews seek him through the Torah. Christians seek him crying, "Abba, Father!" yearning for what they feel.
Who is God?
The devout molds himself in the image of the God he craves. The atheist molds himself in the negative of the image he rejects. The rebellious molds himself in the image of the God he fears. The oppressor molds all by controlling the image of his God.
Who is God?
We need to know.
The lonely cry out and He answers. The hungry cry out and He feeds. The lost cry out and He leads. But who is God? Dare we step beyond the immediacy of our needs to know this God for who He really is? Not for what He can do for us, but for His very being?
What if God left His imprint, not just in us, but in the pages of the Bible? The image of the Creator left at the scene of creation? Would it be worth the study? It would take maturity, courage, and suspension of our disbelief. It would require an open mind and ready heart.
Are you ready for your graven images to crumble?
Who is God?
You are about to find out.

James Bryson
Writer, Writing Coach, Engineer, and Friend

Introduction

"God is in control." I was taught this all my life. But then a respected Bible college professor challenged me, pointing out that if God is in control, then He is the one killing babies right now. If He is in control, then He is the One causing war and spreading diseases. There is no way around this. If God is in control then He is responsible.

Think about this. It may be easy to maintain the idea that God is in control if you are sitting in your comfortable easy chair, sipping a nice cup of tea, but put yourself in the shoes—if they have any—of the millions of people who right now don't have enough to eat. Or imagine you are being tormented month after month with suicidal thoughts. Or imagine that you were one of the countless numbers of Iraqis under Saddam Hussein's rule who had their hands tied behind their back and then from that binding rope were suspended from a ceiling in a dark underground cell.

Perhaps, as I have, you have faced situations in life which have left you wondering about God. How is God involved in this world? To what degree is He orchestrating the affairs of humankind? How much is He responsible for and how much has He left in our hands? Maybe, as I have, you have come across Bible passages which talk about God's dealings with this world, and they have left you wondering—even troubled.

I was troubled enough to start over. Convinced that the God of the Bible is the true God, I decided to rebuild. I started in the book of Genesis and built one truth upon another. In a short time, I was seeing God as I had never seen Him before. I was seeing Him in a way that contradicted the image I had been taught in Church, through most Christian books, and in the three seminaries which I attended. My study of the Bible shook my concept of God.

What became obvious was that we Christians in the Western world have inherited from our Church fathers a concept of God distorted by ancient Greek philosophy. That distorted concept was built like a house of cards and removing one of many cards can make that house crumble. One of those cards is the doctrine that the future already exists. That may sound strange to you at this point, but as you read on you will learn how the Church's traditional understanding of God all rests on this doctrine. If this one doctrine, which originated with the ancient Greek worldview, is removed, then our concept of God will be shaken, and hence, the foundation of Western theology will shift.

This is what I want to show you in the pages to follow. In Part I, we will look in the Bible to see how God has revealed Himself. Beginning in Genesis 1:1, and then progressively moving forward, we will develop a simple, yet clear, concept of God from the biblical revelation.

In Part II, I will explain how the historic Church developed its concept of God relying heavily upon philosophical thought.

In Part III, you will see how these two concepts of God vary and how they cannot be reconciled.

In Parts IV through VII, I will discuss the profound implications. First, we will examine how our concept of God determines how we understand His involvement in our daily lives. Second, I will explain how our concept of God determines what we think about ourselves. Third, we will examine how our concept of God lies at the foundation of our Christian doctrines and everything we believe. Finally, we will see how our concept of God determines our understanding of the nature and origin of death, evil, and suffering.

My end goal is to show you how the implications of your concept of God reach into every doctrine, every church, every home, every prayer, and into every decision you make. If you change your concept of God, your entire worldview will be shifted—and hopefully, by the end of this book, God will be more real and accessible to you.

Part I
The God of the Bible

The Bible is the written record of God's dealings with this world and His interactions with humanity. In the Holy Book we have over 2,000 years of documentation concerning those interactions along with the thoughts of various individuals and their understanding of the ways of God. Contributing to those thoughts are some of the most influential people in human history, such as Abraham, Isaac, Jacob, Moses, Samuel, Elijah, David, Solomon, Isaiah, Daniel, Matthew, Mark, Luke, John, Peter, and Paul. Their understanding of God has been preserved and passed on to us so successfully that today it is the book in more homes and hearts than any other book in human history.

Let's look in that Book to see what is revealed about God—His ways and His nature.

I will start in the beginning. From time to time, I may jump ahead in the Bible to passages that add more to our understanding of the characteristic about which we are learning, but I will attempt to build one truth upon another as God is progressively revealed in the Holy Pages.

Chapter 1
Almighty Creator

Determined to build an understanding of God upon what the Scripture reveals, let's start with the first verse of the Bible:

> *In the beginning God created the heavens and the earth.*
>
> (Gen. 1:1)

From this verse we can know that God is the Creator. We can also conclude that God was around before this world existed. He preexisted the heavens and Earth. Many other verses confirm this and even assure us that God is eternal, that is, He always was and always will be (*e.g.,* Gen. 21:33; Ps. 41:13, 90:2; Is. 40:28).

I wonder what God was doing in eternity past. Was He creating other worlds or thinking about us? The Bible tells us little to nothing about God's actions or state before He created this world. Many Church leaders have warned of the futility of such conjecture. Augustine, Luther, and Calvin each made reference to a well-known statement whose origin is unknown: "God was preparing hell for those who pry too deep." What was He doing? We do not know. Our written revelation of God starts: *"In the beginning. . . ."*

The second verse in the Bible tells us:

> *. . . the Spirit of God was moving over the surface of the waters.*
>
> (Gen. 1:2)

This reveals an aspect of God called the Spirit, and that Spirit can move in space. Often people envision God filling the whole universe at every moment. Perhaps other Bible verses will lead us to that conclusion as we continue; however, here we must note that God's Spirit can be in a certain location in relation to Earth.

And He can move about.

A more observant Bible student may be able to identify some additional facts about God from these opening verses, but to me, these are the ones that seem the most obvious—undeniable.

The next facts are revealed as God creates things by speaking them into existence.

> *Then God said, "Let there be light"; and there was light.*
>
> (Gen. 1:3)

He speaks! And when God speaks, things come into existence: light, stars, plants, animals. . . God is powerful!

The power of God is an aspect of His nature which is prominent throughout Scripture. He created the universe with His spoken Word, destroyed humanity (except Noah and his family) with a flood, repeatedly rescued the Hebrew people from their enemies, worked miracles through Jesus, resurrected His Son, and, in the end, will consummate all things in Christ Jesus.

To help us understand the power of God, it is helpful to examine the related name by which He is known: *El Shaddai,* which commonly is translated as "God, the Almighty One."

To understand this name for God, it is important to

know that Hebrew words are closely tied with the function which is being communicated. The term *El* refers to God, but it would be misleading to interpret *Shaddai* as "the Omnipotent One," because the word "omnipotent" is too impersonal.

In Genesis 17:1, we read about God appearing to Abraham and declaring that He is *El Shaddai*. In that context, God was communicating to Abraham in a very personal way. The root, *Shad,* is associated with the Hebrew word for breast, and therefore, *Shaddai* may be interpreted as "the Abundantly-Breasted One." Hebrew scholars also would be comfortable interpreting *El Shaddai* as "God, the All-Sufficient One."

The point is that in order to translate Hebrew words accurately, careful attention must be given to function and context. If we were to interpret *El Shaddai* as "God, the Omnipotent One," we would be saying something that the Hebrew word is not actually saying. The word omnipotent does not communicate too much, but rather it communicates too little. It does not convey God's heart for people. God was not interested in revealing that He is the "All-Powerful One." He was interested in making Himself known to Abraham—and us—as Provider, Shelter, Giver, Life, and all we need.

As we continue, I will use the word "Almighty" as a characteristic of God, but I hope you will keep in mind the relational aspect that was communicated in the Hebrew language.*

---

* For a different perspective, yet enlightening discussion on the difference between "Almighty" and "Omnipotent" see John Sanders, *The God Who Risks* (Downers Grove, IL, 1998), p. 188-194.

Who Is God?

To this point in our study we can state that God is the Creator and He is eternal. There is a Spirit aspect of His nature which can move about over Earth. He speaks, and when He speaks, things come into existence. God is powerful and almighty!

Chapter 2
God's Love and Vulnerability

On the sixth day of Creation, God made Adam and Eve. We will discover several eye-opening truths concerning this in the next chapter, but here note God's personal involvement with the creation of people. He breathed into Adam (Gen. 2:7). Elsewhere the Bible tells us that God is the Father of the spirits of all flesh (Num. 16:22; 27:16; Heb. 12:9).

This leads us to the question, "Why?" What was God intending for humankind? What motivated God to create humanity? Why didn't He go on eternally existing without us? Did He know what He was getting Himself into?

Numerous Bible verses indicate that, indeed, He did know. Perhaps the most profound verses along this line are those referring to the Father's plans to send a Redeemer (*e.g.*, Acts 2:23). Before God created this world, He made provisions for what He knew was ahead—even the sin of humankind.

I have to compare this with my own situation as a parent. Before my wife and I had children, we did not know what we were getting ourselves into. We had an idea from glimpses of how other parents dealt with their children. However, we never knew how intertwined our lives would become with our daughter and two sons. We did not know that years later, even after they grew up and left home, that our emotional well-being would remain so dependent upon their welfare. It does not matter how distant they

11

are. If they are doing well, then our lives are better. If they are suffering, then we are hurting. They even hold a certain authority over our lives, with the ability to hurt or bless us. I had no idea this would happen.

Perhaps God's relationship to us is not as a parent's relationship to his or her children. God could have created the world without making Himself vulnerable. He could have set everything in motion and then backed away, letting it run without His further involvement or concern. Yet that scenario does not fit the further revelation we have of God throughout Scripture. For example, we are told that in the days of Noah, God saw how sinful people had become and He was grieved that He had made humanity (Gen. 6:6-7). If we take this literally, then we must recognize that God experienced disappointment.

As we continue in our study, we will see many other passages in the Bible which reveal how God remains very much involved and intensely concerned about us. Further, the truth of God's ongoing vulnerability is consistent with the revelation we have of God through Jesus Christ. Certainly the heart of God is revealed as the Word became flesh and dwelt among us. Our Lord laid aside His divine nature and even died for us. Having this revelation of the nature of God, we should not be surprised that in Creation He also made Himself vulnerable.

Perhaps before this world was created God existed independently and totally fulfilled in Himself. But when He created us and became the *"Father of the spirits of all flesh"* (Num. 16:22; 27:16; Heb. 12:9), He opened Himself for relationship with us.

God must have known what He was getting Himself into. That is amazing. He knew ahead of time, yet decided to proceed with His plans. He created us even though He knew that it would cost Him personally.

That causes me to see Creation as an act of love. I used to think that the death of Jesus was the greatest demonstration of God's love. Now I see Creation as equally great, for the decision to create us included the decision to sacrifice for us. Creation is not a huge game, nor is it simply a project on which God is working. He is invested in this universe and in us. Creation is, in fact, an expression and demonstration of His love.

Indeed, God is vulnerable in relationships, and He loves.

Chapter 3
God's Image And Likeness

Then God said, "Let Us make man in Our image,
according to Our likeness. . . ."

(Gen. 1:26)

We see in this verse a correlation between God's nature and ours. We are created in God's image. In some ways we are as God. This implies that we can look at people and get an idea of God's nature.

That is wonderful and revealing, but also sobering!

We know, of course, that humanity fell into sin, and hence, what we see in each other today may be different than what was seen in our original parents. Yet, we must not think of ourselves as totally estranged from God's image, because other Bible verses indicate that we still bear His image. For example, after Noah's flood, God gave a warning that no one is to kill another person, since we all are made in His image (Gen. 9:6). The New Testament agrees, for Paul explains that every person *"is the image and glory of God"* (I Cor. 11:7; see also Jas. 3:9). The inescapable truth is that humans—even after the fall—are still God's image-bearers.

To what degree are we similar to God?

Great thinkers in Church history have often noted that humans are similar to God in the sense that we were created to rule over Earth as God rules over all. Certainly that is one aspect of our image-bearing nature, but there must be more.

Paul inferred more when he talked with the philosophers and other leaders in Athens. He explained:

> *Being then the children of God, we ought not to think that the Divine Nature is like gold or silver or stone, an image formed by the art and thought of man.*
>
> (Acts 17:29)

Paul was examining the nature of humanity and from this he drew conclusions about the nature of God. He was making the argument that God is more like us than He is like a man-made statue. Since we are living, Paul inferred that God is living.

In what other ways are God's nature and our nature similar?

We must be careful in asking this question. If God has declared that we are made in His image, and then we immediately question, "In what way?" we may be imposing our doubts upon His declaration. Consider the seriousness of questioning God in this manner. We read the statement that we are made in His image, and then our minds ask: "Are we as He is in our physical bodies? Are our hearts as His? Are our emotions as His? Does He have hands and feet? Does He have a brain such as ours?" In each and every one of these questions, we have narrowed the truth of God's statement. We are looking for only a part of our beings to resemble Him, rather than believing that, indeed, we are made in His image.

I am not implying that God and we are indistinguishable. Nor am I suggesting that God has a physical body, as we do. Instead, I am resisting the tendency to do what I have seen done by many other individuals studying the natures of God and humanity. In reverence to God, they immediately minimize humanity's existence. Of course, God is greater than we are, but let's simply believe the Bible as it is written. We are made in His image, not just in one aspect of our beings—but our beings. You and I are made in God's image.

Furthermore, we can see a correlation between God's nature and the male and female genders of humanity:

> *God created man in His own image, in the image of God He created him; male and female He created them.*

(Gen. 1:27)

From this we can infer that the image of God is not expressed fully in only the male, nor is God's image revealed in the female alone. Somehow there is a more complete expression of the nature of God in the creation of both male and female.

This is not a book about male and female roles; however, we cannot learn about God without our discoveries having a profound impact upon our theology and lives. For example, if we accept that both male and female came forth from God, then we must conclude that both are good. Furthermore, together they express the nature of God.

I find this significant for my own marriage. Years ago when I got married, I tended to think of a man as being more in the image of God than a woman. I was not conscious of this way of thinking, but it was rooted

17

in my concept of God being male, and hence, women being slightly less in the image of God. As a consequence, I entered into marriage with an attitude that I needed to bring my wife to my way of thinking in every area. Through the years I have learned that God is expressed more perfectly through our lives together as my wife and I become one in heart and mind.

This has implications for every area of human relationships. The fact that the nature of God is expressed in both male and female implies that if we suppress the expression of one or the other gender, then we are suppressing the nature of God in the world. This has implications not only for relationships within the family unit, but also for business, government, church, and all affairs of life.

Hence, we see that our understanding of the nature of God has profound implications for how we govern our lives.

Chapter 4
The Giver of Blessings

God blessed them; and God said to them, "Be
fruitful and multiply, and fill the earth, and
subdue it. . . ."

(Gen. 1:28)

After God created Adam and Eve, He blessed them. He
did not give them a list of rules and regulations. He did
not punish them. He did not scare them. He did not hurt
them. God extended kindness and expressed His good
intentions toward them.

It is helpful to know what God defines as blessings:
being fruitful, multiplying, filling, and subduing.

Many people are confused about this. They think they
are blessed, when, in reality, they are neither fruitful
nor successful. They consider themselves blessed, even
when they are experiencing pain, poverty, barrenness,
and bondage.

This issue is so important that it is worth identifying
the opposite of God's blessing, that is, a curse. If we examine the results of the sin of Adam and Eve, we see that
the ground is no longer fruitful, but Adam must work by
the sweat of his brow to get it to produce. Childbearing
is no longer easy, but filled with pain. Rather than Adam
and Eve ruling over all the affairs of life, Adam rules over
Eve, and Satan gains some authority over humankind.

This distinction between blessing and cursing is a
fundamental principle seen throughout the Bible. God
declared to the Hebrew people that if they obey Him,

then they will be blessed. Those blessings are not merely mystical feelings of well-being, but God listed tangible things: the abundance of possessions, victory over their enemies, good health, numerous offspring, a good reputation, lending rather than borrowing, and leading rather than following (Deut. 28:1-14).

In contrast, God warned the Hebrew people that they would be cursed if they did not obey Him. He outlined some of those curses, including poverty, sickness, confusion, defeat, famine, drought, fear, wayward children, family discord, marital turmoil, slavery, and bondage (Deut. 28:15-68).

This is not to say that God is not blessing the poor and oppressed. There are many examples in the Bible of God helping those under terrible circumstances. Furthermore, we know that in our own lives God blesses individuals in the midst of difficulties. However, it is the general principle of the blessing versus the curse which I am identifying. God's blessing yields fruitfulness, multiplying, filling, and subduing.

Furthermore, God's intentions are to bless humankind. James wrote:

> *Every good thing given and every perfect gift is from above, coming down from the Father of lights, with whom there is no variation or shifting shadow.*
>
> (Jas. 1:17)

God is the ultimate Source of good.

This is confirmed through the revelation of Jesus Christ. God so loved the world that He gave His Son.

Jesus came that we might have life and have it abundantly (John 10:10). This was the purpose of His coming to Earth. Hence, we know that God is not up in heaven unconcerned, or worse, wanting to hurt us. He wants to bless us. That is who He is.

Chapter 5
God Is Relational, Social, and Personal

As we continue our study from the beginning of the Bible, it quickly becomes evident that God desires relationship with us. In the Garden of Eden, God walked and talked with Adam and Eve. He had relationship with them. When Adam and Eve sinned, the relationship changed, but God gave His promise of a coming Messiah, making provision for a renewed relationship.

Throughout the Old Testament, we learn of God's continued dealings with humankind, especially His patience toward the Hebrew people. Then, in the New Testament we see the great demonstration of His love, as He sent His Son to die and reconcile humanity to Himself. Finally, in the end, we have the vision wherein God will spend eternity with His people. The obvious characteristic revealed about God is that He cares about us and wants to be involved with us.

God is relational and social.

Please recognize this as a true characteristic of His nature. When we talk about a specific human being, we often will describe him or her as either social or reclusive. We may explain that one person is outgoing and fun loving, while another person is introspective and a loner.

As we identify the characteristics of God revealed in the Scripture, we recognize that He repeatedly reaches out to us and desires to have relationship with us. God is not a Creator who started the world and left humankind to run things, while He watches from a distance. The Bible reveals to us a God who wants to be involved with us.

Furthermore, His involvement is personal. This is revealed even more when we consider God's interaction with Cain and Abel. When they brought their offerings to the Lord, God's response was eye-opening:

> *And the Lord had regard for Abel and for his offering; but for Cain and for his offering He had no regard.*
>
> (Gen. 4:4b-5a)

God had different responses to these two brothers.

This reveals an important truth. When God looks at us, He sees individuals. Some people wrongly envision God's relationship to humanity as they would think of a human looking at an ant mound, not distinguishing one ant from another. That image is erroneous. God is involved and interactive. He not only distinguishes "one ant from another," but He watches over and cares for each of us individually. He knows us intimately.

The Psalm-writer declares:

> *O Lord, You have searched me and known me.*
> *You know when I sit down and when I rise up;*
> *You understand my thought from afar.*
> *You scrutinize my path and my lying down,*
> *And are intimately acquainted with all my ways.*
>
> (Ps. 139:1-3)

Many other Bible passages declare similar truths. God

looks into the heart of every person (*e.g.,* I Chron. 28:9). He knows us by name.

Yes, God is relational, social, and personal.

Chapter 6
God Shows Favor

Genesis 5:24 tells us that *"Enoch walked with God."* This implies that other people in that time period were not walking with God. Chapter 6 of Genesis adds that *"Noah found favor in the eyes of the Lord"* (Gen. 6:8). The implication is that there were other people not finding favor with God.

This contradicts some people's image of God. They think of God sitting up in heaven emanating love, much as the sun floods Earth, without respect to whom or on what that light pours down. Yet, if we are going to believe the revelation of God in the Scripture, we will see Him as responsive and interactive with individuals. Of course, Scripture says that God *"causes His sun to rise on the evil and the good"* (Matt. 5:45). This means that God gives every person provisions, opportunities, and blessings, but it does not mean that He treats everyone the same nor gives everyone the exact same benefits.

Consider Saul when he had his conversion experience on the road to Damascus. He was traveling city to city in order to persecute and even kill Christians. As he was traveling with a group of men, a great light flashed and God spoke to him. Note that God did not speak to nor call all of the men traveling with Saul. God chose Saul and renamed him Paul.

God can show mercy to whomever He chooses to show mercy. He does not have to treat every human being the same. He can choose any individual to do whatever He wants, whenever He wants. And He does.

Sometimes He sovereignly decides to treat an individual in a unique fashion even though they have done nothing good or bad (Rom. 9:11-13). In other situations, God gives certain individuals special benefits because of some action to which He responds. For example, Psalms 147:11 tells us:

> *The Lord favors those who fear Him,*
> *Those who wait for His lovingkindness.*

Note the conditions on which God's favor is gained.

Consider David, who won a special place in God's heart. In contrast, we can note God's attitude toward certain evil people:

> *The Lord abhors the man of bloodshed and deceit.*
>
> (Ps. 5:6b)

> *And the one who loves violence His soul hates.*
>
> (Ps. 11:5b)

Some Christians cannot accept God's varying attitude toward individuals. Their sun-like, love-bathing concept of God causes them to wrongly interpret certain Bible passages. For example, in several passages we are told that *"God shows no partiality"* (some translations interpret this phrase as "God is no respecter of persons"). Christians often interpret this phrase to mean that God gives favor equally to every human being. In reality, that is a distorted interpretation of the no-partiality phrase.

Let's take a short detour to examine the Bible passages

which tell us that God shows no partiality. Romans 2:9-
11 states:

> *There will be tribulation and distress for ev-*
> *ery soul of man who does evil, of the Jew first*
> *and also of the Greek, but glory and honor*
> *and peace to every one who does good, to the*
> *Jew first and also to the Greek. For there is no*
> *partiality with God.*

Notice that God's absence of partiality has to do with
people being Jew or Greek. In that sense, He will not
favor one person over another. Yet, the context of this
passage is talking about judgment. God judges. Some
people will experience tribulation and distress, while
others experience glory, honor, and peace. God will judge
all, Jew and Gentile.

Peter had a similar revelation:

> *"I most certainly understand now that God is*
> *not one to show partiality, but in every nation*
> *the man who fears Him and does what is right*
> *is welcome to Him."*
>
> (Acts 10:34b-35)

In this passage we are told that God will not favor Jews
over Gentiles. All are welcome to Him, regardless of
their race.

Let's consider additional places in the Bible where the
no-partiality phrase is used.

> *But from those who were of high reputation*

> *(what they were makes no difference to me; God*
> *shows no partiality) . . . .*
>
> (Gal. 2:6)

God is impartial toward the social status of individuals, whether they are great or small, famous or unknown, master or slave (see also, Eph. 6:9).

The no-partiality concept is also presented in the Old Testament. In Deuteronomy 10:17-18, we are told that God will not be influenced by those who offer bribes. He executes justice to all, orphan or widow, alien or native.

It is interesting to note that almost all of the Bible passages which use the no-partiality phrase are talking about judgment. Judgment entails choosing one person over another. God does this. His judgment will not be based on one's ethnicity nor status in life. In that sense, He does not show partiality. However, He does and will show partiality. In fact, He actively is searching to find those to whom He can show favor.

> *For the eyes of the Lord move to and fro*
> *throughout the earth that He may strongly*
> *support those whose heart is completely His.*
>
> (II Chron. 16:9a)

Chapter 7
What Pleases God?

Now that we recognize that God does not treat each person with the same regard, let's take a few minutes to consider the basis on which His favor may be gained.

For example, Hebrews 11:6 tells us:

> *And without faith it is impossible to please Him. . . .*

Faith pleases God. People who do not have faith are not pleasing to God. In fact, it is impossible for them to please God.

I want to please God. Don't you? The Apostle Paul explained:

> *Therefore we also have as our ambition . . . to be pleasing to Him.*
>
> (II Cor. 5:9)

In making this statement, Paul was encouraging all Christians to endeavor to please God. There are things which you and I can do to give Him pleasure; having faith is one of them.

This contradicts some Christians' views of God. As I previously described, they think of God as the sun, evenly bathing all people with love and favor. Furthermore, some Christians misunderstand the gospel message to mean that once a person is saved, God will see nothing other than Jesus, and, therefore, every Christian appears the same in God's eyes.

That is untrue. God loves His children, but just as a parent can be pleased with the behavior, attitudes, accomplishments, and life-styles of their individual children, so can God. He experiences varying degrees of pleasure with His children, depending upon what they do and how they behave.

Humility is another quality that garners God's favor. We are told that *"God is opposed to the proud, but gives grace to the humble"* (Jas. 4:6). James wrote this to Christians, reminding them that God treats individuals differently, and, in part, it corresponds to our being humble before Him.

Further, we can say that God recognizes and likes our good works. We know that our salvation is based on grace through faith, rather than the works of the Law, but God still likes it when people do good things (Heb. 13:16).

In the book of Acts, we are told about a man named Cornelius whose life-style was pleasing to God, and, hence, he won God's favor. Cornelius, we are told, was:

> . . . *a devout man and one who feared God with all his household, and gave many alms to the Jewish people and prayed to God continually.*
>
> (Acts 10:2)

In the verses following the description of Cornelius, we learn about an angel which appeared to Cornelius, saying:

> *"Your prayers and alms have ascended as a*

memorial before God."

(Acts 10:4b)

God took notice and we are told specifically what caught His attention: prayers and almsgiving.

There are other Scriptures which imply that God favors some people over others because of who their parents are. For example, God declared that He extends His lovingkindness to thousands of generations after someone who loved Him (Ex. 20:5-6). Similarly, King David was noting the actions of God when he wrote:

. . . I have not seen the righteous forsaken
Or his descendants begging bread.

(Ps. 37:25)

We can conclude from such verses that God blesses differently, that is, He gives some people greater benefits than others, based upon whether or not He was pleased with their parents, grandparents, and others who have gone before them.

So, God does show partiality. As we saw earlier, it is not based upon being Jew or Gentile, rich or poor, orphan or widow, slave or free, famous or unknown. However, God does show favor to individuals because of certain attitudes or behaviors they express in their lives.

Some readers may react to what I am saying here because of an implication which they know is unavoidable. Many who hear that God shows favor may move into a "performance" sort of Christianity. This is a special concern for Christians who have worked hard to grasp that God loves them just as they are. Yes, God has consuming love for each one of His children. Furthermore, our salvation is given by grace through faith. However, it is also true that there should be some performance orientation to our lives. As Paul said, he made it his ambition to be pleasing to the Lord (II Cor. 5:9). Paul was oriented to perform in ways which pleased the Lord.

Notice how our concept of God determines how we should live. If we think of God as the sun, evenly bathing all people with the same favor, there is little motivation for people to try to please Him. On the other hand, if God is responsive to individuals, then there are things we can do to give Him pleasure. The point is: *You* can please Him!

Chapter 8
God Is an
Emotional Being

Returning to our progressive search through Scripture to discover the nature of God, we next can say that He is emotional. I do not say this in the sense that He is immature or unbalanced. However, even a casual reading of Scripture reveals a God very much moved to and by emotional feelings.

Think of God's reaction when He looked down upon the wickedness of humanity in the time of Noah:

> *The Lord was sorry that He had made man on the earth, and He was grieved in His heart.*
> (Gen. 6:6)

God felt sorrow; He grieved.

On the other end of the spectrum, I can point out how God rejoices over His people (Is. 62:5) and takes pleasure in their obedience and prosperity (Deut. 30:9; Ps. 35:27).

Some of the most startling expressions of God's emotions revealed in Scripture are centered around His reactions to the sins of humanity. While the Hebrew people were wandering in the wilderness, Moses went up on the mountain to meet with God. During the absence of Moses, they made and worshipped a golden calf (Ex. 32:1-8). Note God's reaction:

> *The Lord said to Moses, "I have seen this peo-*
> *ple, and behold, they are an obstinate people.*
> *Now then let Me alone, that My anger may*
> *burn against them and that I may destroy*
> *them . . . ."*
>
> (Ex. 32:9-10)

God got angry. He was so angry that He was ready to utterly destroy the Hebrew people. (God later changed His
mind, which we will discuss in subsequent chapters.)

Consider what God did when the Hebrew people
grumbled because there was no meat available to them
in the wilderness. God became angry and said:

> *"You shall eat, not one day, nor two days, nor*
> *five days, nor ten days, nor twenty days, but a*
> *whole month, until it comes out of your nostrils*
> *and becomes loathsome to you . . . ."*
>
> (Num. 11:19-20)

Not only did God give them more meat than they could
possibly eat, but while it was still in the people's mouths,
God struck them with a severe plague, from which many
of them died (Num. 11:33-34).

I do not want to sound irreverent when I say this, but
God's actions in this passage are disturbing. If a personal
friend of mine acted in such a fashion, I would be shocked
and question the appropriateness of his or her actions.
Since we are talking about God (who is always just and
right), we have to realign our thinking accordingly.

The God of the Bible experiences anger, and that
anger influences His decisions, actions, and behavior.

In the passage we just read, His anger was stirred not only by the people's desire for meat, but also by their complaining. We are told that God's anger *"burned"* and was *"kindled greatly"* (Num. 11:10). The fact is that there are numerous Bible passages which talk about God's anger.

It is also interesting to note that on some occasions it takes time for His anger to subside. After the ordeal with the golden calf, God told Moses to take the people into the Promised Land without Him. God explained:

> *". . . I will not go up in your midst, because you are an obstinate people, and I might destroy you on the way."*
>
> (Ex. 33:3)

God was angry enough to destroy His people. Have you ever been so angry at someone that it became necessary to separate yourself from them for a season? God has been that mad. In fact, it took some time for His anger to dissipate.

Even though I am pointing out examples of God's anger in the Bible, my aim is to show that God has emotions—a full array of them, and often very strong ones—which influence His behavior. This is part of who God is.

The implications of this characteristic of God are far-reaching. When we adjust one aspect of our theology, other areas also have to shift. When we acknowledge the emotional side of God's nature, we must recognize it as good. What, then, does that say about the emotional makeup of a human being?

In the culture of which I am a part, as a North American

Christian, we often look negatively on emotions. We are especially critical of people who allow their emotions to strongly influence their behavior. Since many of us have envisioned God as unemotional, we have tended to think a stoic life-style is more spiritual and godlike.

In reality, the biblical view of God leads us to the conclusion that emotions are okay. In fact, people who completely suppress their emotions are not healthy. I am not trying to validate every emotional or impulsive action, nor am I trying to address the issue of when or in what cases people's emotions are good. I am simply saying that people who show no emotions are not godlike.

As I have become more aware of the emotional and social facets of God's nature, I have realized that God is more similar to us than I previously had thought. I have reconsidered the implications of the fact that we are created in His image. Of course, God is infinitely greater than we are, and I do not want the comparison I make to be misunderstood. However, I now believe that God is more similar to us than most of us have allowed ourselves to recognize.

Chapter 9
God Is a
Covenant-Maker

The next characteristic of God which we discover in the Scripture is His willingness to enter into covenant relationships with people. This means that God is not only willing to relate to people, but He is willing to enter into deeper, committed relationships. We can compare this to a person who is willing to have friends, but he is also willing to get married to the right individual. In a parallel fashion, God is willing to commit.

The book of Genesis reveals that He made covenants with Adam and Eve, Noah, Abraham, Isaac, and Jacob. There are others in the Scripture, yet the covenant established with those who believe in Jesus Christ over-shadows all of the other covenants.

Unfortunately, people, especially in the Western world today, do not have the same understanding of covenant as people did in Bible days. When we learn about God entering into covenant relationships with humankind, we consciously and subconsciously filter that concept through our worldview. If we think of a covenant through the eyes of a Westerner, we tend to think in legal terms and envision God making a solemn contract.

In contrast, the Hebrew people in biblical times had a much more relational understanding of covenant. When two parties entered into covenant with one another, they were committing themselves to make decisions together and work through the problems of life with each other.

They would share the same friends and enemies. Their possessions would be available to one another. Covenants were seen as lifetime commitments and typically extended benefits to the descendants of the covenant partners.

Two individuals in covenant are "insiders." They know personal things about each other. Those outside of covenant relationship are treated differently. For example, with the New Covenant which we have through Jesus Christ, God forgives our sins and breathes His desires upon our hearts (Heb. 8:10). People outside of that covenant cannot share in the same intimacy (this is another example of how God shows partiality, treating people in covenant with Himself differently than those outside of covenant).

To see the difference between a legal understanding of covenant and a relational understanding, consider marriage. The marriage covenant is not meant to be a legal arrangement as much as it is a heart commitment of two people investing their lives in one another. People with a Western mind-set often misunderstand this. Hence, when one marriage partner does something which displeases the other, the second may take an offense and treat the former as a legal opponent. In reality, the relational covenant is the commitment to never treat one's partner as an opponent. The two are to work with each other, side by side. They are committed to make decisions together and for the benefit of one another.

This relational understanding of covenant—which is the biblical understanding—influences our understanding of how God relates to us.

An excellent example of how God views covenant is

seen in His dealings with Abraham. He conferred with Abraham before destroying Sodom and Gomorrah. God said: *"Shall I hide from Abraham what I am about to do. . . ?"* (Gen. 18:17). Knowing he had a covenant with God, Abraham dared to reason with God: *"Wilt You indeed sweep away the righteous with the wicked?"* (Gen. 18:23b). God honored His covenant with Abraham and allowed him to enter into the decision-making process.

Compare this with how the marriage covenant is meant to establish a relationship between two people. In my own marriage, I would be wrong to spend any significant amount of money or make a major decision without allowing my wife to be involved in the decision-making process. Marriage partners are supposed to cooperate and work with each other.

It is only when we accept this covenant-making aspect of God's nature that we can understand many of His actions as recorded in the Bible. For example, there are several biblical accounts where we see God expressing His anger with His people. However, on more than one occasion God allowed His covenant-partner, Moses, the privilege of reasoning with Him and, thus, talk Him out of destroying the people (*e.g.,* Ex. 32:11-14). The fact that God allowed Moses the honor of influencing His actions is directly related to God's covenant-keeping nature.

God is open for dialogue and He can be influenced in His decisions.

The Western, contractual understanding of covenant tends to obscure this relational aspect of God's nature. Misunderstanding the covenant relationship, people may demand God to measure up to whatever He has promised in His Word. With a Hebrew understanding, we realize that such demanding for legal justice is unnecessary, and, in fact, wrong. To demand God to fulfill His part of a bargain is to misunderstand what a covenant is, since it entails approaching God from a legal point of view rather than a relational one.

Compare this idea with marriage. If a husband demands certain behaviors from his wife, based on the legality of their binding marriage contract, the relationship is robbed of honor. To treat a covenant partner in a legal way is an insult. In fact, it is a violation of that covenant, because a relational covenant is an agreement to treat the other person as a bonded mate, rather than as a legal opponent.

Here is the good news: God is a Covenant-Maker and a Covenant-Keeper. Those who enter into covenant with God are entitled to a deeper relationship with and closer access to Him. God includes His covenant-partners in His purposes, plans, decisions, and actions. He honors them and considers their input.

Furthermore, a covenant entails commitment. Even if we are unfaithful, He remains faithful to His commitment (II Tim. 2:13).

Chapter 10
God Changes His Mind

The implications of God being a Covenant-Maker are profound—too wonderful to fully grasp. Among other things, it means God will listen to His covenant-partners.

Look carefully at how Moses dialogued with God after God declared that He was going to destroy the Hebrew people.

> *Then Moses entreated the Lord his God, and said, "O Lord, why does Your anger burn against Your people whom You have brought out from the land of Egypt with great power and with a mighty hand? Why should the Egyptians speak, saying, 'With evil intent He brought them out to kill them in the mountains and to destroy them from the face of the earth'? Turn from Your burning anger and change Your mind about doing harm to Your people. Remember Abraham, Isaac, and Israel, Your servants to whom You swore by Yourself...."*
> (Ex. 32:11-13)

Moses reasoned with God. The most amazing thing is God's response.

> *So the Lord changed His mind about the harm which He said He would do to His people.*
> (Ex. 32:14)

God *changed His mind.* Yes, *God* changed His mind.

This is not the only place in Scripture where we read of God deciding to do one thing and then altering His course in response to people's actions and prayers. Another incident is when God told King Hezekiah that he was going to die. In response, Hezekiah cried out to God for mercy, and, indeed, God added 15 years to Hezekiah's life (Is. 38:1-6).

Consider, also, how God changed His mind from destroying the city of Nineveh after they repented in response to the preaching of Jonah.

> *When God saw their deeds, that they turned from their wicked way, then God relented concerning the calamity which He had declared He would bring upon them. And He did not do it.*

(Jon. 3:10)

It is important to note that God changed His mind; however, He did not change in nature. The theological word used to refer to this unchanging nature is *immutability.* Understanding the immutability of God, Jonah later prayed:

> *". . . for I knew that You art a gracious and compassionate God, slow to anger and abundant in lovingkindness, and one who relents concerning calamity . . ."*

(Jon. 4:2)

In relenting from His planned destruction, God was

acting consistently with His nature, being Someone who is abundant in lovingkindness (see also, II Sam. 24:16; Jer. 18:7-8).

It is reassuring to know that God never changes in character. James tells us of the goodness of God and reassures us that this aspect of His nature will never change.

> *Every good thing given and every perfect gift is from above, coming down from the Father of lights, with whom there is no variation or shifting shadow.*
>
> (Jas. 1:17)

In the book of Malachi we read God's words:

> *"For I, the Lord, do not change . . ."*
>
> (Mal. 3:6)

In both of these passages, God is reassuring His people that they can trust Him because He will remain the same kind of Person throughout eternity.

This is good news. We do not have to worry that (at some point in the future) God will change and become evil or unpredictable. Even after a million years, He will continue to be good, and, in fact, the Ultimate Source of good. When we recognize this quality of God, we should see it as attributed to His nature. However, we must not say that God is immutable in His decisions, for He can and does, at times, change His mind.

There is one passage in the Bible which has been used wrongly by some Christians to teach that God will never reverse His decisions. It is a verse from the book of I Samuel where the Prophet Samuel was rebuking King Saul. Samuel was speaking of God's attitude toward the king when he said:

> ". . . the Glory of Israel will not lie or change His mind; for He is not a man that He should change His mind."
>
> (I Sam. 15:29)

Some have concluded from this statement that God never changes His mind. In the context, however, we see that Samuel had just told the king that God had rejected him. Even though King Saul cried out for mercy, Samuel was telling the king that in this case God would not change His mind. Furthermore, God was not as a man who can be forced or bribed into changing His mind.

However, in the previously discussed passages of Scripture, we learn that God can and does change His mind. Further we can note that God often deals with nations in such a fashion, as He explained through the Prophet Jeremiah:

> "At one moment I might speak concerning a nation or concerning a kingdom to uproot, to pull down, or to destroy it; if that nation against which I have spoken turns from its evil, I will relent concerning the calamity I planned to bring on it."
>
> (Jer. 18:7-8)

It is important to note that the changes God makes involve more than His mind or thoughts. His entire attitude with people can also change at some point in time. For example, Isaiah explained God's dealings with Israel.

> *But they rebelled*
> *And grieved His Holy Spirit;*
> *Therefore He turned Himself to become their*
> *   enemy,*
> *He fought against them.*
>
> (Is. 63:10)

Notice that God turned, He changed His attitude or disposition toward the people because of their rebellion.

God is not an immovable Being, unaffected by humankind or events. He does, indeed, respond to us.

In summary, we must be careful and say that God is immutable in nature, but not in emotions, thoughts, decisions, nor attitudes toward individuals.

Chapter 11
God Is Sovereign

Even though Abraham dared to reason with God about the destruction of Sodom and Gomorrah, he approached God from a position of humility and great respect. Moses, too, spoke to God, not with an attitude of demanding change, but rather he entreated and reasoned with God, hoping God would respond.

Further study of God's dealings with humanity reveals how He rules from a position of authority high above this world. After King Nebuchadnezzar was humbled before God, he declared:

> *"All the inhabitants of the earth are accounted*
> *as nothing,*
> *But He does according to His will in the host*
> *of heaven*
> *And among the inhabitants of the earth;*
> *And no one can ward off His hand*
> *Or say to Him, 'What have You done?' "*
>
> (Dan. 4:35)

God is the Supreme Ruler in such a fashion that He does not have to answer to any higher authority. God is sovereign, meaning He can do whatever He wants to do, whenever He wants to do it.

With a recognition of God's sovereignty, it is time to make a transition. It is time to compile and examine the list of characteristics about the nature of God which we have thus far developed.

The Nature of God:
Creator
Eternal
Has a Spirit Which Can Move About
Speaks
Creates by His Word
Powerful
Almighty
Vulnerable
Loving
Living
Encompasses Male and Female
Giver of Blessings
Source of All Good
Relational
Social
Personal
Shows Favor to Individuals
Takes Pleasure in Individuals
Emotional
Covenant-Maker
Changes His Mind
Immutable in Nature
Sovereign

We could continue reading through the Bible and discover many additional truths about God, but already the list we have compiled has several characteristics which contradict the view of God commonly held by Christians in the Western world. Readers trained in theology will immediately recognize those contradictory points. Most other readers probably have been following my study of

Scripture and have had no problem embracing each of these characteristics as biblically accurate and true to the nature of God. In reality, the view which I have thus far developed is in direct conflict with the view held by the historic Church and most of Christianity today.

In Part II of this book, I will explain the view of God commonly held by the Church and show how it differs from the view we have thus far developed from Scripture. Then in Part III, I will explain why these two views cannot be reconciled with one another.

Part II
A Philosophical
Concept of God

How and why is the traditional concept of God different than the one I outlined in Part I? To answer this,
we need to delve into philosophy and Church history. I
am not a philosopher, but I can communicate in simple
terms the highlights which have fashioned the modern
Western view of God.

Chapter 12
The Philosopher's Understanding

If we go back to the Greek philosophers who lived 500 to 300 years before Jesus, we find Socrates, Plato, and Aristotle. Historians know that these great philosophers, and those surrounding them, established the fundamental thought patterns of the Western world. They developed the basic concepts of logical thinking, and they are accredited with what is identified today as the ancient Greek worldview. This profoundly influenced European thought and eventually became rooted throughout the entire Western world.

Socrates (ca. 469-399 BC) focused on the question, "How can we know?" He used his mind to challenge logically every idea and assumption that he could. So unsettling was his questioning to the society in which he lived that government officials sentenced him to death after accusing him of leading the youth astray.

Plato (ca. 427-347 BC) followed Socrates and continued to ask questions. Most significant to our discussion is the fact that Plato asked questions related to God. During his lifetime, the majority of the Greek people believed in many gods, such as Zeus, Artemis, Poseidon, and Aphrodite. Plato did not blindly accept those beliefs, but concluded that there must be some supreme God who is self-existing. By self-existing, he meant that there must be some God who exists without being created. Plato referred to that self-existing one as "the Good." Although his concept of the Good was not of a personal Being as Christians understand, but this was the closest thing which he had to our concept of God.

Aristotle (384-322 BC) built on this foundation and he, along with other philosophers, began to refer to the Good as the "Immovable Mover."

Ancient Greek Philosophers' Concept of God:

Immovable Mover

This concept of the Immovable Mover came from the idea that the Self-Existing One is too great and too big to be moved by creation. This characteristic of God became known as *impassibility,* referring to how God is never passive in the sense that things can act or move upon Him. Instead, God is so powerful and magnificent that He is moved by nothing while He acts on everything.

The early philosophers also argued that the Immovable Mover must be "perfect." They went on to define perfect as being without lack or in need of anything. From this idea, the early philosophers reasoned that if the Immovable Mover changed from its state of being perfect, then it would no longer be perfect. Therefore, it is impossible for the Immovable Mover to ever change. To refer to this unchangeable aspect, they used the term *immutable.*

The word immutable also described their God, because they equated the Immovable Mover with truth. Since truth never changes, the Immovable Mover could never change.

One other significant characteristic which the early philosophers assigned to God is *timelessness.* This concept emerged from the Greek philosophical worldview which saw time as a trap in which the natural world is confined. Thinking of God as perfect, the philosophers could not accept the idea that God was confined to the limits of time. Therefore, they conceived of God as existing outside of time and filling all of time. Our earliest records show that it was Aristotle who first used the term timelessness, meaning God is so free from the limitations of time that there is nothing related to time in His nature

The concepts of timelessness, impassability, and immutability are inseparably linked. If God fills all of time, there could never be anything new come to His attention. From eternity past, He would have known how you and I were going to act today. Therefore, it would be impossible for Him to ever change His mind or have an emotional response to our daily activities. If God fills all of the time, then He is impassable and immutable.

It is these points which became the foundation of ancient Greek philosophical thought concerning God:

- Timeless
- Impassible
- Immutable

As we continue, we will see how these points are in conflict with the revelation of God which is given to us in the Bible. In particular, the implications that God can never have emotional responses nor change His mind are diametrically opposed to the biblical revelation of God. As we will see, the ancient Greek philosophical concept of God varies from almost every point which I developed from a direct study of Scripture in Part I.

Chapter 13
Augustine's Concept of God

Several early Church leaders introduced the ancient Greek concept of God to Christianity, but Augustine (354-430 AD) was the most influential. To see this we need to know that before becoming a Christian, Augustine was a student of Plotinus (ca. 205-270 AD). Plotinus was a non-Christian philosopher who had taken the writings of Plato and reworked them into what is called Neo-platonism. Plotinus referred to God as "The One" and explained how God is above all human understanding. Further, Plotinus taught that for a human to see God is as gazing at the sun because truth, goodness, and beauty radiate out of "The One" more brilliantly than light from the sun.

Plotinus' Concept of God:

THE ONE

This was the concept of God which Augustine had when he began investigating Christianity. However, Augustine was unable to fully embrace Christianity because of the numerous verses in the Bible which talk about God changing His mind and showing emotions. He was so committed to his philosophical concept that God was immutable, that the idea of God changing his mind or showing emotions was an "absurdity." In his book entitled *Confessions,* Augustine explained how he was unable to accept the Scripture as divinely inspired until he heard Ambrose, the Bishop of Milan (340-397 AD), allegorize the Old Testament and explain as mere figures of speech the verses which talk about God changing.* According to Bishop Ambrose those verses were anthropomorphisms—the Bible writers' attempts to explain God in human terms. Augustine embraced this explanation and rejected the literal biblical accounts of God changing His mind and showing emotions.

After he became a devout and influential Church leader, Augustine was able to instill his way of thinking into the Church partly because of the significant point in history in which he lived. Preceding the fourth century, Christians were persecuted and thousands were martyred for their faith. Then in the year 313 AD, Constantine, the emperor of Rome, passed a law granting religious freedom. Soon Christianity became the official religion of the Roman Empire, and hundreds of thousands of people flooded into the Church. The vast majority of those people were of the Greek and Roman culture. Facilitating

---

* Augustine, *St. Augustine's Confessions I,* Loeb Classical Library, Book VI, p. 285.

this sudden and massive expansion of Christianity were Church leaders such as Augustine.

Although I am focusing on the key role Augustine played in establishing the Western understanding of God, it is worth noting that the Christian world was ripe for his teachings. All of the church fathers had been wrestling with the issues of introducing Christianity to the Greek and Roman worlds. The Greek culture was dominant throughout that region. The Jews who lived outside of Israel had embraced the Greek culture to such an extent that they needed a Greek translation of the Old Testament rather than the original Hebrew used by their forefathers. That Greek translation was called the *Septuagint.*

Today when we read the Septuagint it is easy to see how the Hebrew Bible was interpreted not only into the Greek language but also through the Greek worldview. Because the Greek philosophical concept of God was of a huge glowing force, many passages were deliberately translated eliminating what the translators considered anthropomorphisms of God. For example, the original Hebrew version of Exodus 24:10 tells about the Hebrew leaders seeing God; the translators of the Septuagint inserted the word "place," saying that the leaders saw the place where God was. In the Hebrew version of Isaiah 38:11, we read about Hezekiah bemoaning the fact that he will not see the Lord any longer; the Septuagint inserts the word "salvation," hence telling us that Hezekiah will not see the salvation of the Lord. The translators of the Greek Septuagint made numerous such changes reflecting their concept of God as the Immovable Mover, who is untouchable and unknowable.

What is important for us to know is that the Septuagint was the principle version of the Old Testament used by the early Church (up until the Latin Vulgate was translated by Jerome in the fourth century). This knowledge helps us understand how the early Church moved away from the ancient Hebrew concept of God (in particular, recognizing changes in God's emotions and decisions) and was strongly influenced by the Greek philosophical view. Through the work of Augustine this change was seated into the theology of the Western Church.

One idea which Augustine further developed was the concept of timelessness. He explained that God exists in the "eternal now." By this he meant that every moment throughout all of time stands immediately before God. He right now exists in the year 3000 BC, and in the present, and in the year 3000 AD. He sees every moment right now as if it were happening before His eyes.

Augustine's View of God–Existing in the Eternal Now:

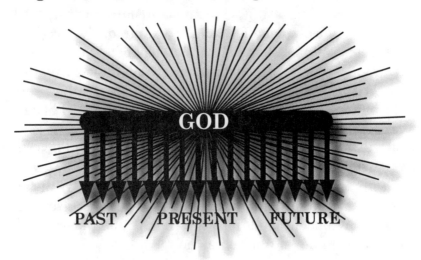

We can appreciate Augustine's great work, however, we should keep in mind that at the very heart of his labor was the attempt to help the Greek and Roman masses accept the God of the Bible as their God. Being a student of Greek philosophy, it was natural for him to present the Christian God in a form which they could more easily embrace. Although Augustine recognized God as a personal Being, to him God had the same fundamental characteristics as the God of the ancient Greek philosophers.

Augustine's Understanding of the Characteristics of God:

- Timeless
- Impassible
- Immutable

Church historians generally agree that Augustine's theology has dominated Roman Catholic and Protestant thought since the fifth century. His concept of God became the commonly accepted view of the Church.

An excellent example of Augustine's influence is seen in the construction of huge cathedrals during the Middle Ages. The places where people met with God were built with massive stones, reflecting the immovability of God. High lofty ceilings testified of His greatness and incomprehensibility. The unemotional and stoic concept of God can be seen in how people approached Him within those cathedrals, taking on a very quiet, reverent attitude. Since they conceived of God as being quiet and stoic, they naturally wanted to take on the same nature when coming into the sanctuary of God.

This concept of God has become known as the Classical View of God. It has been held by most of the historic Church since the time of Augustine and it profoundly influences the thoughts of most Christians today.

Chapter 14
The Classical View of God

In the Middle Ages, many Christian philosophers and theologians followed in the footsteps of Augustine further developing the Classical View of God. During that period, philosophy was primarily thought of as "faith seeking understanding." The logical arguments of philosophy were seen as supporting theology, and hence, philosophy and theology were seen as inseparable and totally compatible.

During the late Middle Ages, significant amounts of Classical Greek writings were translated and made available in Latin, the common language of the educated population throughout most of Europe. Aristotle's works became the most popular among these. In fact, Aristotle's influence was so predominant he was simply referred to as "the Philosopher."

Drawing heavily upon Aristotle's writings, Thomas Aquinas (1225-1274 AD) is known for battling the philosophical issues of his time. Aquinas is most remembered today for his logical arguments on the existence of God. However, it is important to know that Aquinas set out to prove the existence of the Immovable Mover. As a result, his efforts established the Classical View of God more firmly in the minds of the Western Church.

The philosophical arguments concerning God were especially important in battling with the non-Christian world. In particular, the threat of Islam was pressing on the door of Christianity during the Middle Ages. Muslim scholars excelled in philosophical thought. This further pressured Christian leaders to rise to meet the serious intellectual challenges and give themselves to a philosophical concept of God.

This period of intellectual endeavor became known as *Scholasticism* (1000s to 1400s), during which time knowledge was thought to increase as thinkers built on the ideas of those who went before them. In particular, they focused on studying, rehashing, and refining the writings of great thinkers such as Aristotle, Augustine, and Aquinas. Eventually, the whole of Europe was being transformed by the founding of universities. Theology and philosophy held positions as king and queen in the kingdom of education. Students were expected to first and foremost master these subjects. By the birth of the Protestant Reformation, more than 80 universities were operating in Europe.

This is the world into which Martin Luther (1483-1546) entered. The God portrayed by the Church at that time was the God who was worshipped by quiet, somber people sitting in massive cathedrals. It is also helpful to know that Luther was an Augustinian monk before he challenged the established Church. Luther's contributions to Christianity are widely known and appreciated, but we must keep in mind that his theology was built upon the same basic philosophical concept of God held by Augustine.

As the Protestant Reformation blossomed, the term *sovereign* came to the forefront. This word, sovereign, was stamped indelibly on their concept of God and came to mean that God is the One who "causes all things."

This definition of sovereign crystallized under the teachings of John Calvin (1509-1564). He taught that "Nothing happens except what is knowingly and willingly decreed by Him [God]."* When Calvin declared that God is sovereign, he was implying that God is the Sole Originator of all that happens in this world. In other words, God is in total control. This is little to no different than the concept of God as the Immovable Mover. God moves all things and nothing moves Him.

The Word "Sovereign" Superimposed Upon the Immovable Mover Concept of God:

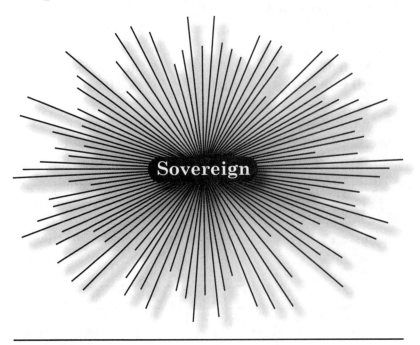

* See Calvin, *Institutes of the Christian Religion,* ed. John T. McNeill (Philadelphia: Westminster, 1960), 1.16.3.

Notice how different John Calvin's definition of the word sovereign is than the definition which I offered earlier (chapter 11). I stated that God is sovereign in the sense that He is the Supreme Ruler in such a fashion that He does not have to answer to any higher authority; He can do whatever He wants to do, whenever He wants to do it. This definition is in agreement with its use in Scripture (and with Webster's Dictionary). We can verify this by noting how the word sovereign is used in the Bible as a characteristic of human kings. A sovereign king is one who can do whatever he wants to do without having to answer to any higher authority. Using this definition of sovereign, we can say that God is sovereign, and by this we mean that God can do whatever He wants to do.

When Calvin stated that God is sovereign, he was implying much more. He was saying that God *is controlling all things* and *is causing all things*. In contrast, the biblically accurate understanding implies that God *can* cause whatever He wants to cause but it leaves open the possibility that God can choose not to control some things. He may sovereignly decide to let many things move according to natural laws or subject to other influences.

From this point forward, I will distinguish between these two definitions by writing the word **sovereign** in enlarged, bold letters when referring to Calvin's all-controlling definition.

	Calvin's View	Biblical View
Attribute of God:	**Sovereign**	Sovereign
Definition:	Controls all things	Does whatever He chooses

As we think seriously about the attributes of **sovereignty,** timelessness, immutability, and impassibility, we realize that these are logically consistent with one another. Reformed theology (Calvinism) is a systematic way of thinking which incorporates all these attributes. The *Westminster Confession of Faith,* which is a document putting Reformed theology into practical usage, declares: "There is but one only, living, and true God, who is . . . without body, parts, or passions. . . ."* This document, which declares that God has no passions (inner emotional experiences), has been the standard statement of faith for thousands of churches and millions of churchgoing people. In reality, the God of Reformed theology was built on the concept of the Immovable Mover with the capstone being the word **sovereign.** It is the Classical View of God in its most rigid form.

---

*Cornelius Burges, *Westminster Confession of Faith,* ed. S.W. Carruthers (Glasgow, UK: Free Presbyterian Publications, 1986), p. 6.

Chapter 15
Sovereignty and Predestination

If we form our understanding of God by imposing the word **sovereign** upon the image of an Immovable Mover, then we will conclude that God causes all things. Furthermore, the predestination of all things is the inescapable, logical implication. God moves everything and He is moved by nothing.

Historical, Philosophical Concept of God, Showing God Causing All Things:

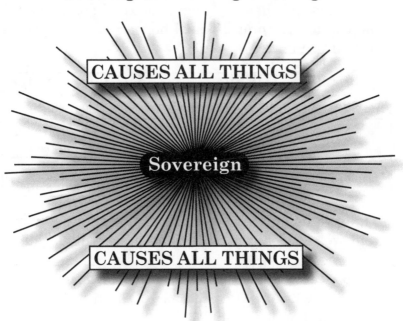

CAUSES ALL THINGS

Sovereign

CAUSES ALL THINGS

Augustine wrote that "the will of the omnipotent is always undefeated."* Thomas Aquinas, Martin Luther, and John Calvin would all agree. Since they each built their theology upon the same philosophical concept of God, the doctrine of predestination permeates their teachings.

In contrast, if we build our theology using the more accurate definition of sovereign (God can do whatever He wants to do), then we will realize that God *can control* whatever He wants to control; He *can intervene* in the affairs of the world whenever He chooses; and He *can predestine* whatever He wants to predestine. However, God is only doing what He wants to do. Many things He allows to move on their own. Many things are under the influence of human beings without God's direct involvement. He has sovereignly decided not to control or predestine all things. This, I hope to convince you, is the Biblical View.

	Calvin's View	Biblical View
Attribute of God:	**Sovereign**	Sovereign
Definition:	Controls all things	Does whatever He chooses
Implications:	All things are predestined	Some things are predestined

Our two definitions of sovereign determine to what extent we see God controlling and predestining things

---

* Augustine Enchiridion 26, in Augustine: *Confessions and Enchiridion*, trans. Albert Outler, Library of Christian Classics Vol. 7 (Philadelphia: Westminster, 1955), p. 400.

in this world (the primary subject of Part IV). Our definition of the word sovereign also profoundly influences what we believe about human nature, the origin of evil, and the cause of suffering (topics we will discuss in Parts V and VII). The implications of these ideas reach into every church, into every home, into every prayer, and into every mind in the Western world.

Chapter 16
The Church's View of God

The modern Church still tends to think of God as the Immovable Mover and to superimpose the characteristics of God upon the image of a huge glowing force. For example, the Bible tells us that God is love (I John 4:8), and therefore, if we have embraced the Classical View of God, it is reasonable for us to envision love radiating out of God as light from the sun. Not every Christian sees God this way, but subconsciously this view impacts all of us.

The Classical View of God:

LOVE

So also with the Classical View of God, Christians tend to envision God's goodness, holiness, glory, righteousness, and justice, all flowing out of God, bathing the universe with the attributes of His nature. Although different teachers emphasize different attributes, the following are usually among those embraced by modern Christians holding to the Classical View of God.

Attributes of God Commonly Accepted by Adherents of the Classical View of God:

Self-Existing (Uncreated)
Timeless (Existing in the eternal now)
Immutable (Unchanging)
Impassable (Not acted upon, which implies
    that He never changes His mind and
    never experiences emotional changes)
Omnipotent (All-powerful)
Omniscient (All-knowing)
Omnipresent (Present everywhere)
Sovereign
Good and Loving
Holy and Glorious
Righteous and Just
Self-Sufficient (Needing/wanting nothing)

Other characteristics could be added here, and we could expound upon these, but this list will be sufficient to expose the most obvious errors of the Western view of God.

Part III
Two Views in Conflict

Christians think they have a biblical view of God, but most have embraced certain Greek-originated, philosophical concepts without knowing it. As a consequence, their theology is inconsistent. The two views—Classical and biblical—cannot be reconciled. To be logically consistent, a person must choose one or the other. Please allow me to explain.

Chapter 17
Different Views of God

Since the fifth century, the historical, philosophical concept of God has dominated the halls of higher education and the thoughts of Church leaders trained therein. This Classical View of God has been held by the historic Church since the time of Augustine, and it continues to hold the minds of most educated Christians in the Western world today.

The Classical View of God:

GOD

On the other hand, there also is a countless number of sincere Christians who hold to a more personal, interactive concept of God. They live their daily lives trying to please God, believing that God is willing to change His mind and engage with them in the give-and-take affairs of daily life. In other words, they hold to a view much like that which I developed in Part I from a direct reading of Scripture.

Let's identify those characteristics in which the Classical View and Biblical View differ from one another. These will be used in further discussion.

Classical View:	**Biblical View:**
Timeless	Eternal
Immutable	Immutable in Nature but Mutable in Decisions and Emotions
Impassable	Responsive to His Creation
Omnipotent	Almighty
Omniscient	Infinite in Knowledge
Sovereign	Sovereign
Totally Self-Sufficient	Has Wants
Invulnerable	Vulnerable
Shows No Favor	Shows Favor to Individuals
Takes No Pleasure	Takes Pleasure in Individuals
Legal Covenant-Maker	Relational Covenant-Maker

Although many theologians have embraced some form of the view which I have labeled the Biblical View—referring to it as the Open View of God*—a majority of Bible scholars continue to hold to the Classical View.

---

* For further study on the Open View of God or what is called, Open Theism, see *Recommended Reading* in the back of this book.

Before we go on to explain and examine the contradictory nature of these two views, it is important to discuss my labels of the Classical View versus the Biblical View. Some readers may object to my use of the terminology "Biblical View," because they hold to the Classical View, and they believe that their view is biblically-derived. I do not want to offend, but the fundamental distinction between these two views stems from how tightly we hold to Scriptural revelation. The Classical View can only be derived from the Bible if one reads it through the lens of historical, philosophical thought.

Typically, the Classical theologian's approach to understanding the nature of God is to study the writings of great theologians who have gone before us. Rather than taking the Bible in hand and drawing conclusions from what it actually says (as I did in Part I of this book), a Classical theologian will talk about the conclusions of Augustine, Anselm, Thomas Aquinas, Martin Luther, John Calvin, Rene' Descartes, and others. Then the theologian will point out the positives and negatives in the arguments of those great thinkers and attempt to address unanswered questions. A Classical theologian who wants to talk about the nature of God is expected to enter into the historic, philosophical dialogue on this subject.

Therefore, the gap between the Classical View and Biblical View is primarily created by what we value as truth. Christians holding to the Biblical View read the Bible and believe it very literally. Theologians holding to the Classical View treasure the writings of the great thinkers throughout Church history and believe that God has been revealing Himself not only through the Bible but also to the historic Church through those great teachers. Therefore, it is unthinkable for them to simply discard the thoughts of those respected leaders.

As with all challenges to well-established beliefs, what is at risk is not only our present understanding but our loyalties to people we respect and honor. To question the foundational assumptions of leaders such as Augustine, Luther, and Calvin is a monumental challenge. Call me arrogant or foolish, but I must join the ranks of those willing to question the great thinkers and accept the God who is revealed from a direct reading of the Scriptures.

Of course, I am not alone in this. Not only are there more and more Christian theologians shifting their views, but the ancient Hebrew people recognized the God of Abraham, Isaac, and Jacob as a personal and inter-active Being who displays emotions and, on some occasions, changes His mind. In contrast, the God of Classical theology who is an Immovable, Immutable, Impassable Mover-of-All-Things would have been unrecognizable to Abraham, Isaac, and Jacob. Please let me explain this more clearly.

Chapter 18
Is God Timeless
Or Eternal?

If God is timeless, as the Classical View tells us, then He exists in the eternal past, the present, and the eternal future simultaneously; all events which have ever happened or ever will happen stand before Him right now. As we explained earlier, if God is timeless, then there never is any new information coming to Him. Therefore, He can never change His mind, nor do His emotions ever rise or fall. If God is timeless, then all of His decisions were made before this world was created and the future is already set. On the other hand, if any of the biblical references to God changing His mind or showing emotional changes are to be taken literally, then God is—at least in some fashion—experiencing time with us.

This distinction identifies a fundamental difference between our two views of God. Note that both views say that God has always existed and always will. But the Classical View of God holds that God right now exists in the future and the past. Since the time of Augustine, most of the Church has embraced the Classical View of God and with it the assumption that God is timeless. In biblical times the Jews and the early Church never believed that God was timeless.* That

---

* For an excellent explanation of how the early Church thought of eternity as unlimited in both the forward and backward directions, see Oscar Cullmann, *Christ and Time,* trans. Floyd V. Filson (Philadelphia, PN: Westminster Press, 1964).

idea did not emerge until Christianity was interpreted through the Greek philosophical worldview.

As I explained in chapter 12, our earliest records reveal that it was Aristotle who first used the term timeless. He and other Greek philosophers equated God with truth and since truth is timeless, they concluded that God must be timeless. I hope you can see the limitations of that reasoning. God is truth but He is more than that. If we recognize Him as a Personal Being, it puts in question the idea of timelessness.

The word timeless is not in the Bible, but we are told that God is eternal (*aionios,* in Greek). Classical theologians like to equate this word eternal with timeless, but that simply reveals their bias to interpret Scripture through their philosophical concept of God.

To confirm this, we can read many Bible passages which show that word *aionios* does not mean timeless. For example, Romans 16:25-26 uses the word *aionos* twice:

> *. . . the revelation of the mystery which has been kept secret for long ages* (aionios) *past, but now is manifested, and by the Scriptures of the prophets, according to the commandment of the eternal* (aionos) *God, has been made known to all the nations. . . .*

In this passage, the first use of the word *aionios* refers to the distant past, even the infinite past, but not timeless. The second use of the word *aionios* is used descriptive of God, but there is no justifiable reason for us to change its meaning in order to equate it with timeless. All we can say for sure is that the descriptive term *aionios* tells us that God is eternal in the sense that He always existed and always will exist.

We also know that *aionios* is not equivalent to the word timeless, because the word, *aionios,* is used in several passages of the Bible when speaking of the life which all Christians possess. For example, I John 5:11 tells us that God has given us eternal (*aionios*) life, and this life is in His Son. The same life which is in Jesus is in us. Therefore, if eternal means timeless, then all Christians are timeless. Yet, even Classical theologians will not say that Christians exist in the eternal past, the present, and the eternal future simultaneously. Instead, we know that Christians have received eternal life, and hence, they will live forever. Using the same definition of the word eternal, we can say that God is eternal, but we have no biblical evidence that God is timeless.

At the same time, every passage that refers to God changing His mind or having emotions that vary is evidence that God is not timeless.

Classical theologians dismiss all of those Bible passages as anthropomorphisms. Yet, it is not that simple to dismiss those Bible passages. When God was angry with the Hebrews and about to kill them, Moses boldly reasoned with God. Perhaps we can dismiss this interchange between God and Moses as an anthropomorphism, but if we do, then we must also say that that interchange between God and Moses never took place. Similarly, when Abraham bartered with God about not destroying Sodom and Gomorrah, we can dismiss that interaction as an anthropomorphism, but then we must also admit that the interchange never happened or God was just pretending to listen to Abraham.

One more of many examples which we can give is of Joshua praying that the sun will stand still; we are told that "... *the Lord listened to the voice of a man*" (Josh. 10:14). If we dismiss this as an anthropomorphism, as Classical theologians must do, then we are saying that God never did listen to Joshua. The point is that if we reject certain passages as literally true, then we must reject many of the related events as ever having taken place. That puts into question our whole understanding of Scripture.

In other words, if we equate the biblical word, eternal, with the word, timeless, and we claim that God is time- less, then we must reject as true not only what Classical theologians call anthropomorphisms of God, but also the corresponding interactions between God and humanity which the Bible tells us actually took place.

Right after the introduction, I started this book with a clear statement concerning the nature of the Scrip- tures:

> The Bible is the written record of God's deal- ings with this world and His interactions with humanity. In the Holy Book we have over 2,000 years of documentation concerning those interactions along with the thoughts of various individuals and their understanding of the ways of God.

If there is any truth to this statement, then we must be careful not to discard as anthropomorphisms the interac- tions between God and man which are recorded in the

Scriptures.

This issue is so key and foundational that it is worth taking another chapter to further investigate.

Chapter 19
Does the Future Already Exist?

Perhaps God exists in a timeless fashion in some other dimension—outside of this universe—we do not know. The Bible does not tell us. The only revelation we have of God is that in our world He shows Himself as if He is experiencing time with us.

Christians trained in the Classical View like to support their view by saying, "There is no time in the realm of the spirit." Yet, if time did not exist in the realm of the spirit, then there would be no time boundaries in that realm. If that were true, then demons could transcend time and go into your past to cause tremendous problems in your present and future life. Also, when judgment day comes and God throws Satan into the Lake of Fire, Satan could escape by moving outside the confines of time. The point is that demons are limited in time, even though they exist in the spirit realm.

Another fundamental characteristic of the spirit realm is that things change. For example, 2,000 years ago Jesus ascended far above all rule and authority. At that point in time He was enthroned above all the universe—things changed. If time did not exist in the spirit world, nothing could change. The obvious point is that things do change and, therefore, time does exist in the spirit realm.

The declaration, *"In the beginning God created the heavens and the earth,"* can be interpreted to mean that God was standing outside of time when He created things, however, that assumes that time is only a characteristic of this natural created realm. As we discussed, time does exist in the spiritual realm. God already may have been in the midst of time when He created this world. We do not know. The Bible does not tell us.

Some Christians conclude that there was no time before the beginning of days in Genesis 1. However, recognizing the beginning of days does not necessarily correspond with the beginning of time. That would be as wrong as saying there could be no time until clocks were made. The passing of days does not create time but merely gives us a means of measuring it.

Even if it is true that God existed outside of time before this world was created, this does not necessarily mean He fills all of time within the created realm right now. A simple comparison we can make is of a carpenter who built a house. Though he existed before the house and outside of the house, we need not conclude that he fills that house. Similarly, God created the universe, but this does not necessarily mean He fills all of time.

Consider the Genesis account of Creation. Picture yourself standing with God in the beginning. Before God created the first day, did He exist in the first day? He could not have existed there because God created the universe out of nothing (*ex nihilo*). The first day did not previously exist and God could not exist in something that did not exist. This same principle applies to every day following the first day. On the first day God could not have existed in the second day, because the second day had not yet come into existence. Following this line of thought, we can see that God does not exist in tomorrow because tomorrow does not exist. The idea that God exists in something which does not exist is absurd.

We can say that God exists in all things that exist, but we cannot say that He exists in the future, because as far as we know the future does not exist.

There are serious problems with the assumption that the future currently exists: for one thing, the future cannot exist without us in it. Do you see what this means? If God is in the future watching what we are going to do in the future, then you and I right now exist in the future. Augustine taught that God exists in the eternal now with all of time standing before Him. But if God has always had all things standing before Him, then all things have always existed.

This same discussion can be had concerning the existence of the past. Classical theology also depends upon the idea that the past still exists.

Some who believe in the timelessness of God will point to studies in physics which have led scientists to believe that time is relative. Indeed, it is a well established fact that as something approaches the speed of light, time slows down. Therefore, if we develop the technology to allow an astronaut to travel at or near the speed of light, that astronaut could travel away from home to some distant point and then return to find people who have aged more than he has. Some have misunderstood this to mean that the future already exists. But, in fact, it means just the opposite. At home, time will not pass and the future will not come into existence, unless that astronaut spends at least some time traveling. The conclusion of science, therefore, is that time is relative—but the future does not already exist.

Classical teachers say that God fills all of time, and in

order to prove this, they like to quote Revelation 1:8:

> *"I am the Alpha and the Omega," says the Lord God, "who is and who was and who is to come, the Almighty."*

Indeed, this is a profound declaration of the greatness of our God. However, does it mean that God presently exists in the distant past and simultaneously in the future? Not necessarily. It is just as reasonable to understand this declaration to mean that our Lord has existed forever (He had no beginning) and He will continue eternally (He will have no end), without any reference to existing simultaneously throughout all of time.

Some readers may think of prophecy as proof that God exists in the future, but knowing the future does not necessarily mean that God exists in the future. (I will deal more with this issue in the next two chapters.)

A passage that is sometimes used to "prove" that there is no time in eternity is Revelation 10:6, which says in the King James Version that *"there will be no more time...."* In reality, this verse is speaking of impending destruction, and if we read the verse in its context, we understand the verse to mean that there will be no more time before the destruction recorded in Revelation chapters 7 through 10 is released. Recognizing this, many translations, such as the New American Standard, translate the meaning of this verse more clearly by saying *"there will be no more delay...."* To confirm this understanding, we can look at Hebrews 10:37 and Habakkuk 2:3, where similar terminology is used. The point is that Revelation 10:6 was not saying that there will be no time in eternity, but rather there would be no more time before destruction comes.

Again, we can say that God may exist in a timeless fashion in a different realm—outside of this universe. No one knows for sure. The revelation we have of God in the Bible shows Him personally relating to humanity and reacting to people's daily activities. Perhaps He is timeless in another dimension, but the Bible does not reveal it. That idea came from ancient Greek philosophy. What we do know is that in this world in which you and I live, God reveals Himself as if He were in time with us. That is the only revelation which we have of God. Everything else is pure assumption founded in the ancient Greek worldview.

This discussion is not merely a vain mental exercise. The implications are profound. If you question the existence of the future, you are questioning the foundation of ancient Greek philosophy. Your eyes will open up to see how the Hebrew people in biblical times understood God. He will become more intimate and interactive with you. Hundreds of Bible passages will become clearer. Like dominoes falling, there will be a series of traditionally-held doctrines that will be revealed like the king who was exposed as naked. Truth will unfold. You will see yourself as a child of God. His love will be more personal. Prayer will be more meaningful. You will even understand differently why Jesus died on the cross. Finally, you will know the answer to the question of the ages; "If God is good, why is there so much suffering and pain?"

We will discuss these and other topics in the folowing pages.

Chapter 20
Is God Omniscient?

If someone if going to attack the view of God which I am presenting in this book (or Open theism), the area they will most likely focus upon is God's omniscience, the attribute which accredits to God the knowledge of all things.

You see, if God is timeless, then He would be omniscient. This is logical because if He exists throughout time, the past, present, and future all are standing before Him right now. However, if God is moving through time with us, then it is possible that there are some things about the future which He does not know.

Hearing this concept for the first time—that God may not know everything—causes great alarm in most Christians. It is such an emotional issue that many Christians will immediately shut down all discussion. To have something so foundational in their own theology challenged is too threatening. They would rather stop thinking about the related issues than consider the possibility that God is not omniscient.

Yet the word omniscient is not in the Bible.

The Bible passage most often used to teach that God knows everything is the following:

> *"Are not two sparrows sold for a cent? And yet not one of them will fall to the ground apart from your Father. But the very hairs of your head are all numbered."*
>
> (Matt. 10:29-30)

Obviously, God knows a lot. But does this passage say that God knows everything? No. When I hear teachers quoting this verse to prove that God is omniscient, I am embarrassed for them because they are reading into the Bible what they want to believe.

The passage which tells us that God knows the number of hairs on our heads is a good example of how God reveals Himself in Scripture in a very personal way. Remember how we discussed (chapter one) the difference between omnipotent and almighty? God revealed Himself to Abraham as the Almighty One, because God wanted Abraham to know that He is Provider, Shelter, Giver, Life, and all Abraham needed. With a similar perspective, we must examine the Scripture about God knowing when the sparrow falls and knowing the numbers of hairs on our heads. It would be wrong to take those verses as proof that God knows everything. What God was communicating to us is that He knows everything about us and everything that concerns us. His intentions were to communicate His interest and love for us.

I have no doubt that God is omnipotent. However, there is no verse in the Bible which says God is omnipotent. Therefore, for me to teach that as doctrine would be communicating something for which I have no biblical proof and which God chose not to reveal.

I have no doubt that God knows every blade of grass on the earth and every molecule on Jupiter. I must reassure you, because some readers may get upset with me at this point and want to defend God. Unfortunately, when people get defensive or angry they tend to misread or mishear what others are communicating. I believe God's knowledge is infinite and infinitely beyond our grasp. The reason I believe God's knowledge is infinite is because there is a Bible verse that declares this:

> *He counts the number of the stars;*
> *He gives names to all of them.*
> *Great is our Lord and abundant in strength;*
> *His understanding is infinite.*
>
> (Ps. 147:4-5)

Still, we must realize that infinite knowledge is not the same as omniscience. To see this, consider just one area of knowledge, such as mathematics. We can say that numbers can go on infinitely. It is easy to accept the concept that God knows all the numbers, and therefore, His knowledge is infinite. Yet, this is not to say that He knows everything. Consider the fact that if you take infinity and subtract a number such as 1,000, you still have infinity left over. To know an infinite number of things does not necessarily mean omniscience.

Yes, God's knowledge is infinite, but there is no verse in the Bible that tells us that God knows everything. At the same time, there are many Bible passages which indicate that He does not know some things.

Consider the promise of God to forget the sins He has forgiven. In several verses God says, *"I will remember their sins no more"* (e.g., Heb. 8:12). Of course, this can be considered a figure of speech, but it is also possible that God can sovereignly decide to remove from His own consciousness the sins He has forgiven. In other words, it is possible that a perfect God can perfectly forget. Maybe we should take His words literally.

The Bible also tells us that God searches the hearts of

people, which implies that God is seeking to discover things that He does not know. Further, God tests people to see what is in their hearts. Concerning Hezekiah we are told:

> ... *God left him alone only to test him, that He might know all that was in his heart.*
>
> (II Chron. 32:31)

Deuteronomy, chapter 8, tells us about God allowing the Hebrew people to wander in the wilderness for 40 years:

> "... *that He might humble you, testing you, to know what was in your heart, whether you would keep His commandments or not."*
>
> (Deut. 8:2)

For another example of this testing to know, consider God's work in the life of Abraham. God told Abraham to kill his own son and offer him as a sacrifice (Gen. 22). In obedience, Abraham took his son up to the mountain and prepared him for the sacrifice, but God stopped Abraham right before he killed Isaac. God spoke through an angel:

> *He said, "Do not stretch out your hand against the lad, and do nothing to him; for now I know that you fear God, since you have not withheld your son, your only son, from me."*
>
> (Gen. 22:12)

God said, "... *now I know....*" Didn't God know before

this? If we believe God's words literally, then we have to answer, "No."

Other Bible verses (*e.g.,* I Sam. 16:7; I Chron. 28:9; I John 3:20) tell us that God can see and know everything in the heart of a person, but how does this fit with the idea that God tests people to see what is in their heart? This is understandable if we consider the possibility that the human heart is able to initiate thoughts and desires. God can see into the heart of every person, but ideas that are not in the heart of a person today may arise tomorrow. Since God is moving through time with us, He continues watching, searching, and testing.

No one knows for certain how the dynamics of God's awareness work, but let me propose a possibility. Perhaps God already knows if you are going to get in a car wreck tomorrow. He knows the exact time, location, and every minute detail of the event. However, it may be that God will still be watching to see what is going to come out of your mouth the instant of the crash. Maybe He has created humanity with a free will and the ability to bring things forth from our own hearts without His predetermination or preknowledge. I am not saying this is true, but it is certainly a possibility because it fits with how we see God dealing with others in Scripture.

We must keep in mind that God is sovereign (He can do whatever He wants to do), and therefore, He can decide to not know certain things. On the other hand, if we say that God is omniscient, *we may be denying His sovereignty—* we are saying that God has to know everything and He has no freedom to decide to not know all things.

Let's look at another example of something which God does not know. Before God destroyed Sodom and

Gomorrah, He sent angels to investigate what actually was going on in those two cities.

> And the Lord said, "The outcry of Sodom and Gomorrah is indeed great, and their sin is exceedingly grave. I will go down now, and see if they have done entirely according to its outcry, which has come to Me; and if not, I will know."
>
> (Gen. 18:20-21)

Does this passage trouble or surprise you? It indicates that God was somewhat aware of the sins being committed in Sodom and Gomorrah, but not entirely. He sent angels to the region to see if, indeed, the people were sinning to the degree He was hearing. God investigated in order that He might *"know."*

It is possible that God withdraws His presence and hides His face from certain evil places such as Sodom and Gomorrah. That is, God chooses not to expose His holiness to evil, and, therefore, He chooses not to make Himself constantly aware of some things. Perhaps He can choose to know anything He wants to know. Perhaps He sovereignly has chosen not to be omniscient.

Finally, think again of our earlier discussions about God changing His mind. There are more than 20 places in the Bible where we are told that God does or does not repent (in Hebrew, *nacham*) of some action. What does this tell us about God? If God knows everything, then what a person does tomorrow or the next day already would be known by Him. If God filled all of time, there never would be any new information available to Him.

If He already knew what every person was going to do, say, or pray, then He never would have the opportunity to respond and change His mind. Since the Bible tells us that God changes His mind, and nowhere does it tell us that He knows everything, we must question the traditionally accepted idea of omniscience.*

Of course, there are some readers who may say that I am splitting hairs unnecessarily. They may say that the examples I have given of God not knowing certain things are insignificant compared with the vast knowledge which God does have. Hence, they would be comfortable ignoring these minor "unknowns" and continue to describe God as omniscient.

I agree that God's knowledge is so vast that it is beyond our comprehension. As I said, He knows every blade of grass on the earth and every molecule on Jupiter. However, to have a biblically accurate understanding of God's nature, we must be careful to use biblical terms. God's knowledge is infinite. That is what the Bible teaches—no less, no more. Yet it is alarming to learn how many Christians will fight for a doctrine which is not in the Bible. They will fight as if God needs someone to defend

---

* There are many open theists who recognize certain unknowns in God's knowledge, yet continue to use the term omniscient as a characteristic of God's nature. They can do this because they have defined omniscient to mean "knowing all that can be known." An excellent book offering this view is *God of the Possible*, by Gregory Boyd (Grand Rapids, MI: Baker Books, 2000). I am going further and actually rejecting the use of this term omniscient, to leave room for the possibility that God may sovereignly choose to not know certain things.

Him. They will fight for something which—whether it is true or not—God chose not to reveal about Himself.

Chapter 21
Does God Know All of the Future?

Does God know everything that is going to happen in the future? Christians raised under the Classical View of God immediately will answer, "Yes!" It only makes sense that if God fills all of time, then He knows everything that is going to happen. However, if we remove from our minds the assumption of timelessness and look in the Scriptures with unbiased eyes, what will we learn?

Certainly, there are some things of which God has foreknowledge. Peter preached about the work of God through Jesus Christ, saying:

> . . . this Man, delivered over by the predetermined plan and foreknowledge of God. . . .
>
> (Acts 2:23)

Such verses assure us that God knew from the foundations of the world what His plan was concerning Jesus Christ (see also, I Pet. 1:20).

Not only is the overall plan of God determined for the future, but certain specific events can also be seen to be foreknown by God. For example, the Prophet Agabus knew by the revelation of the Holy Spirit that a famine was to come (Acts 11:28). Since God reveals to His prophets certain events that will happen in the future, God must know beforehand that those events will happen.

However, recognizing that God knows some things

does not mean that God knows everything about the future. Furthermore, it is unclear whether God knows those future events because He has foreknowledge, or because He has sovereignly decided to accomplish the related events. Let me explain.

The words of Amos are enlightening concerning how God works with prophecy in a "foredeclarative" manner.

> *Surely the Lord God does nothing*
> *Unless He reveals His secret counsel*
> *To His servants the prophets.*
>
> (Amos 3:7)

This verse tells us that God is not just foretelling prophets the future, but He is telling them what He is about to do. This is not merely foreknowledge, but "foredeclaration" or "foreordination."

Please note this distinction because it influences how you understand God and prophecy. Amos 3:7 tells us that prophecy is God revealing to us what He is about to do, not foretelling events as if He already had watched them happen.

Another point worth considering is how much God knows because He can see what will arise from the seeds already growing in the hearts of people. Since God watches hearts, He can see what is coming forth. For example, in Old Testament times God warned the Hebrew people of what their enemies were about to do, but we do not know if this was because God already knew the future or because He simply was watching the enemies plan things in their secret chambers. God can see the consequences of people's thoughts, desires, plans, and behaviors. This would give Him the ability to know many things which inevitably will happen.

Looking at things in this light, we can say that God does have foreknowledge of many things. However, it is important to point out that there is no verse or passage in the Bible which indicates that God knows everything about the future. That idea is not taught anywhere in Scripture. At the same time, there are several Bible passages which indicate that God does not know all things about the future.

An interesting example of this is recorded in the book of Jeremiah when God was discussing with the prophet the evils which Israel had been committing.

> *Then the Lord said to me in the days of Josiah the king, "Have you seen what faithless Israel did? . . . I thought, 'After she has done all these things she will return to Me'; but she did not return. . . ."*
>
> (Jer. 3:6-7)

If we take these words of God literally, then we must conclude that God expected the people of Israel to repent, but they did not. This surprised God! This means God did not have complete foreknowledge.

Another example from the book of Jeremiah is when God rebuked the people who had been worshipping false gods:

> *"They built the high places of Baal that are in the valley of Ben-hinnom to cause their sons*

> *and their daughters to pass through the fire to*
> *Molech, which I had not commanded them nor*
> *had it entered My mind that they should do this*
> *abomination, to cause Judah to sin."*
>
> (Jer. 32:35)

God said the people were doing things which had never entered His mind (see also, 7:31; 19:5). If we accept God's words here, then we have to conclude that God does not have complete foreknowledge.

There also are positive things for which God is watching the hearts of people.

> *For the eyes of the Lord move to and fro*
> *throughout the earth that He may strongly*
> *support those whose heart is completely His.*
>
> (II Chron. 16:9a)

According to this verse, God is looking. He does not have perfect foreknowledge. He is watching to see what people are going to do.

This whole concept of God watching to see what we are going to do is assumed when we speak of God changing His mind. If God already knew everything which we are going to do, then He could never change His mind concerning us. Since the Bible clearly gives us examples of God changing His mind, then we cannot escape the logical conclusion that He does not have perfect foreknowledge.

We can also refer again to Bible passages about God arriving at new information. As I discussed in the previous chapter, God tested Abraham and then said, *". . . now I know . . ."* (Gen. 22:12). Similarly, God sent angels down to Sodom and Gomorrah to find out if the sins about which He was hearing actually were happening (Gen. 18:21). If we take these Bible passages literally, then we must conclude that God does not have complete foreknowledge.

There is a Bible passage often used by teachers who want to try to prove that God has perfect foreknowledge. It is Isaiah 46:9-10:

> *". . . I am God, and there is no one like Me,*
> *Declaring the end from the beginning*
> *And from ancient times things which have not*
>   *been done,*
> *Saying, 'My purpose will be established,*
> *And I will accomplish all My good pleasure.'"*

If we read these verses through a mind-set which assumes that God is timeless, then we will conclude that God has perfect foreknowledge. On the other hand, if we avoid that assumption and simply embrace this passage exactly as it is written, we will note that God "declares" the end from the beginning. Declaring does not necessarily mean He has foreknowledge as if He has already seen it happen. It is just as reasonable to say that God is declaring the future because He is deciding to make it happen.

Indeed, Isaiah 46:10 is foredeclaration, and we can verify this if we simply read the very next verse:

> *"Truly I have spoken; truly I will bring*
>   *it to pass.*

I have planned it, surely I will do it."
(Is. 46:11)

As I mentioned earlier, God has had a plan from the foundations of the world, and He is working out that plan in a step-by-step fashion. Therefore, He knows much of what will happen because He is orchestrating those events, causing them to take place.

In summary, I can say that there is no verse telling us that God knows the future perfectly, nor that He already has seen the future happen. Conversely, there are many passages indicating that He does not know everything about the future.

Chapter 22
God Takes Risks, But Makes No Mistakes

More biblical evidence that God is moving through time with us is how He took certain actions and then later was grieved that He had taken those actions. For example, the wickedness of humanity was so great in the days of Noah that the Bible tells us:

> *The Lord was sorry that He had made man on the earth, and He was grieved in His heart.*
>
> (Gen. 6:6)

Another example is how God anointed Saul king over Israel and then later regretted that He had made Saul king (I Sam. 15:11). How could God regret an earlier decision if He filled all of time? It would be impossible. According to the Classical View of God, examples such as these are figures of speech, not to be taken literally. If, however, we accept these Bible passages literally then we have to reject the Classical View of God.

This brings up another question: Can God make mistakes? If He truly grieved about choosing Saul, did He make a mistake in choosing him? We know that God was able to see into the depths of Saul's heart, however, if people truly have a free will and God does not exist in the future, then God did not have complete and total foreknowledge of what Saul would do in the future. Certainly God knew that it was possible for Saul to turn evil. Therefore, God was taking a risk by putting Saul in that position of authority. Does that mean God made a mistake in choosing Saul? No. To give someone a chance is not a mistake.

Compare this with parents who allow their teenager to take the family car out for a drive. That teenager may have an accident, and later the parents may regret the decision they made to let their teenager drive the car. However, that does not mean that they made a mistake. When people are given freedom, there is always a risk involved. It is not a mistake to take a risk and give people a chance.

I do not mean to imply that God is as in the dark about the future as parents may be about their children. God knows every possible scenario and the hearts of all people. His wisdom is infinite and He makes decisions based on information which we cannot possibly grasp. However, as long as He allows people to have true freedom, He is taking some risk by allowing them to act.

We can even consider Jesus. He was "tempted." The very idea that Jesus was tempted means there was a possibility that He could have given in. Therefore, God took a risk in sending Jesus.

The Classical View of God allows no risks on God's part. The Biblical View of God reveals that He is great enough to deal with all situations which may arise. He is not threatened by people having a free will. He is able to work all things—including human mistakes—together for His glory. In this sense, *the God of the Bible is bigger and greater than the God of the Classical View.* Please meditate on this point because it is profound.

Chapter 23
Because of Relationship, Covenant, and Love

If we reject the idea of timelessness and perfect fore-knowledge, then we are saying that God has some limitations. Scripture is unclear whether He is limited by His own nature or if it is simply the result of His decision. Perhaps He simply has decided not to fill all of time or know everything. But why would He do this?

It is possible that He has chosen to limit Himself for the purpose of relationship with us. Certainly, He has chosen to forget our sins so that we can fellowship with Him. Yet, maybe His desire for relationship goes further than this. Perhaps it is the reason He has chosen not to be omniscient. Maybe it is for us.

You see, if God existed throughout time and knew everything already, we never could influence His decisions. It would be impossible for people ever to enter into meaningful dialogue with God with any hope of ever changing His mind. This truth is inseparable from the idea of covenant. As I explained, true covenant entails involving covenant partners in the decision-making process. If God already had everything figured out, it would be impossible for Him to enter into true covenantal relationship with us.

Furthermore, if God filled all of time, it would be impossible for Him to empathize with us or respond to us; nor could He experience hope. He could never experience the joy of watching us grow, or anticipate our responses to Him.

Perhaps, then, it is because of His love, because He is relational, because He is a Covenant-Maker, and because He is sovereign, that He is not impassible or omniscient.

It is the love of God which also leads us to question the Classical idea that God is "totally self-sufficient," needing nothing and wanting nothing. Perhaps before God created this world or before He created any individuals, He existed without any needs or wants. Perhaps in eternity past He existed totally self-sufficient. However, He fathered humanity. God chose to create individuals whom He could love. True love gives, but it also wants. God wants us to do good. He wants to bless us and He delights in the prosperity of His people (Ps. 35:27). God takes pleasure in seeing us succeed.

More importantly, God wants our hearts. In fact, in the context of warning His people not to worship other gods, He declared that He is a jealous God (Ex. 20:5). By definition, jealous means that God experiences emotional anguish when His people turn away from Him.

The Classical View of God cannot accept this idea of God experiencing anguish or any feelings related to us rejecting Him. Teachers would prefer to say that God is a jealous God, not because He truly experiences jealousy, but because we need a jealous God. Classical teachers would also say that God could not experience anguish as a result of our turning away from Him because that would make Him dependent upon us and no longer totally self-sufficient.

Yet the Bible does not tell us that God is self-sufficient in the sense of needing or wanting nothing. That idea came from Greek-originated philosophical thought—not the Bible. The biblical revelation shows us a God who is very much invested in His people. God not only loves His people, but He is "in love" with them. By this, I mean He has yielded Himself to the dynamics which become established when one individual loves another. When He fathered humanity and then further when He entered into covenant relationships, He opened Himself for the dynamics of relationships. Perhaps He was, indeed, totally self-sufficient in eternity past, but the God who reveals Himself in Scripture shows Himself very much involved and intimately responsive to His people.

This is the concept of God which is consistent with the revelation of God in Jesus Christ. In coming into the world, Jesus emptied Himself, and hence, limited Himself. He then became vulnerable to humanity. He hurt. He made this great sacrifice in order to come to us and restore relationship with the Father. Knowing that the heart of Jesus is the heart of God, we should not be surprised that God may limit Himself.

In summary, we can say that God is neither timeless, nor impassible, nor omniscient, nor **sovereign**, nor totally self-sufficient, nor invulnerable. . . because He is relational, He is a Covenant-Maker, He is sovereign, and He loves us.

Part IV
What Is God Doing?

Some readers may mistake this writing as a defense of the Open View of God. That is not my intent. I am trying to read the Bible and believe what it says about God. In that endeavor, I have come to agree with the Open View of God, but not all open theists would agree with every point that I am trying to make. Open theists challenge the attributes of timelessness, immutability, and impassibility. I agree that those attributes are purely philosophical assumptions and have no biblical basis, but I am taking liberty to discuss the implications as I understand them.

From here on I will focus on the underlying concept of the Classical View of God which is the Immovable Mover. That image came from Plato and Aristotle. I am also trying to uproot the concept of a huge glowing force which underlies today's Western concept of God. That idea is seen in the writings of Plato and Aristotle, but it became fixed in Western thought as Augustine drew on the teachings of Plotinus. Plato, Aristotle, and Plotinus were non-Christians—even heathens whose life-styles openly mocked Christian values. Yet, their concepts of God have impacted the minds of Western Christians, distorting Christian doctrine and our understanding of God.

In this section we will see how the Immovable Mover image has distorted our understanding of God's ongoing involvement in this world. In the discussion which follows, I hope to guide you to a realization of how profoundly this image of God is influencing your thoughts, hopes, plans, and daily activities.

Chapter 24
Determinism Versus Openness

The Classical View of God lies at the foundation of Western Christianity, however, through the years many Christian teachers have doubted various implications of that view. In particular, they have doubted the impassibility of God and its implication that God experiences no emotional changes. There have also been many leaders—most notably those who followed Arminian theology—who have doubted the implication that everything is predestined. Still, it is worth noting that even Arminianism is built on the ancient Greek philosophical concept of God. It still sees God as being timeless.

The Biblical View which I am presenting is not Arminian theology. It is not built on the Classical View of God. It rejects the very foundation laid down by the ancient Greek philosophers. It starts with the Bible and builds one truth upon another as it is revealed in Scripture.

This view is most at variance with Reformed theology. As I explained earlier, Reformed theology (Calvinism) is Classical theism in it most rigid form. Reformed theology clings to the idea that all things are predestined, even who will spend eternity in heaven and who will spend eternity in hell. Adherents say that God has pre-appointed every event in every person's life, from birth to death. They believe that God has determined every trial, sickness, and death that we individually face. Because they believe God is so tightly orchestrating the affairs of this world they are called "determinists."

In contrast, the Biblical View which I am endorsing supports the idea that God has a plan which He has been orchestrating throughout the ages, but Creation functions with some level of autonomy. It is running according to natural laws, but God is sovereign in the sense that He can and does intervene whenever He chooses. People have a free will, but God can guide, influence, direct, and even take control whenever He desires. Also, Satan is a created being with some autonomy, though God puts limits on his activity. Furthermore, God is guiding all things in one direction for one end: the ultimate consummation of all things in Jesus. However, within this general direction, God is working with humanity, and much of what happens in the future will be determined by a cooperation between God and humanity.

In reference to God's ongoing activity in this world, I have come to agree with Open theism, because it sees God as open for our input, and, therefore, the future is somewhat open—not yet totally fixed.

Determinism	Openness
God predestined everything.	God is guiding all things toward the fulfillment of His goals, but some things are unfixed.

Most Christians hold to a view of God which is not consistent with either Determinism or Openness. They vacillate between both views, depending upon the topic they are discussing. However, Christians who have thought through the issues will gravitate to and remain fixed on one or the other, depending upon the concept of

God which they believe.

What you believe on this issue will determine how you understand God and His relationship to you. We will examine these implications in the pages to follow.*

---

* Readers familiar with theology may want to note that Open theism is different than Deism, because Open theism sees God as active in this world, rather than standing back and letting all things run only according to natural laws.

Chapter 25
God Is in Charge

A common saying among Western Christians today is, "God is in control!" In reality, this statement is nowhere in the Bible. It is a Christian cliche stemming from the Greek philosophical concept of God.

If we say that God is in control, then we are saying that God is causing all of the suffering and pain in this world. If we say, as John Calvin did, that "Nothing happens except what is knowingly and willingly decreed by Him,"* then we are implying that God is the cause of all things, including all war and disease. If we say that God has exhaustive control of everything, then we are saying that He is the ultimate cause of every baby that dies.

In reality, God is not controlling everything in this world. What the Bible reveals is that God has all authority, and that authority has been given to Jesus (Matt. 28:18). Jesus sits on a throne at the right hand of God (Mark 16:19). He has the power to *subject all things to Himself* (Phil. 3:21). However, we should be careful to recognize that having authority and power is not the same as controlling everything. When a person has authority and power, they can choose whether or not to use that authority and power to take control.

The Bible teaches that Jesus *"must reign until He has put all His enemies under His feet"* (I Cor. 15:25). At the present time, Jesus reigns but He still has enemies. There

---

* John Calvin, *Institutes of the Christian Religion,* ed. John T. McNeill (Philadelphia: Westminster, 1960), 1.16.3.

are people and demons not doing His will. The day will come when Jesus will exert His authority and power. Then every knee will bow and every tongue will confess that Jesus Christ is Lord. Then Jesus will fill all and be in all (I Cor. 15:25-28). For now, Jesus reigns, but He is not controlling all things.

This is confirmed when we note that God does not want anyone to perish, but desires all to come to repentance (II Pet. 3:9). Yet, we know that not all people will be saved. In this respect, His desires are not being met, nor is His will being accomplished. People do many things contrary to the will of God. Many people are living in rebellion to Him. Satan is also wandering the Earth, seeking to destroy people's lives. God sets limits on Satan's activities, as we see in the testimony of Job's life (Job 1:12; 2:6). It is apparent that God limits evil in this world; however, evil is still real, and it may move in opposition to the will of God.

Therefore, it is wrong to say that God is in control. However, that phrase may be used correctly in certain situations. For example, a Christian woman who is governing her life to the best of her ability according to the will of God should have confidence that God is leading and guiding her in her daily affairs. Therefore, when things seem to be going wrong, she can reassure herself that God is in control. She can say this because God will always work things together for good for those who love God (Rom. 8:28). Therefore, if a Christian is going through a difficult situation, she may confess that God is in control of a specific situation. This statement is true so long as the hearts of those involved are in tune with Him.

However, as a general, all-inclusive statement, it is

wrong to say, "God is in control." We can say, "God is in *charge*." God has authority and power to do whatever He desires, and He will use His authority and power whenever He chooses.

Determinism	Openness
God is in control.	God is in charge.

We can also say that God intervenes in the affairs of this world. However, please note that the idea of God intervening is not synonymous with God controlling. If He is in control, then it would not be necessary for Him to intervene. Yet, even a casual reading of the Scripture reveals a God who has intervened many times in the affairs of humanity.

For this reason we are instructed to pray:

> *"Your Kingdom come.*
> *Your will be done,*
> *On earth as it is in heaven."*
>
> (Matt. 6:10)

We pray for God's will to be done on Earth because, at present, God's will is not being accomplished fully on Earth.

A day will come when Jesus commands everything into submission to His will. Then His will shall be done throughout all of Creation. Until that glorious day, many things remain out of control.

Both deterministic and openness Christians agree that God has a predetermined plan which He will accomplish.

However, they disagree as to how detailed that plan is and how forceful He is in executing it. The deterministic Christian believes God is in control of everything, down to the minutest detail. In contrast, the openness Christian sees God inspiring, guiding, directing, and even forcefully intervening at times; however, people have much freedom within the parameters God sets.

Chapter 26
God Is
Working with Us

The Open View of God sees that He is watching us, responding to us, and working with us.

An eye-opening example of this interaction between God and humanity can be seen in one incident when God became angry with the Hebrew people:

> *For the Lord had said to Moses, "Say to the sons of Israel, 'You are an obstinate people. . . . Now therefore, put off your ornaments from you, that I may know what I will do with you.'"*
>
> (Ex. 33:5)

God told the people to repent and wait until He made up His mind as to what action He was going to take. God's response contradicts the determinist's view. It is not possible to accept God's comment literally while clinging to a belief in the predestination of all things (or a belief in the Classical View of God).

The testimony of Esther in the Old Testament provides us with another example to support the openness concept of God and how He relates to us. Esther was the Queen of Babylon at the time when King Ahasuerus reigned. Unaware that Esther was Jewish, the king was deceived into believing that the Jews were rebellious and should be eliminated from his kingdom. So King Ahasuerus issued a decree that on an appointed day the Jews throughout the land would be killed (Esth. 3). Queen Esther knew that she and her people were in danger of being annihilated, but she did not know what to do to stop the actions of the king's decree. Then her uncle Mordecai spoke to her and said:

> *"For if you remain silent at this time, relief and deliverance will arise for the Jews from another place and you and your father's house will perish."*
>
> (Esth. 4:14a)

As a leader of the Jews, Mordecai knew that God would rescue the Jewish people: "Deliverance will arise!" Mordecai knew that God would be faithful to His covenant with them. However, Mordecai also understood that Esther's involvement in this deliverance was optional. Mordecai told the queen that God would deliver, but if she did not speak up then she would be killed, and God would simply choose someone else to use.

That reveals to us a profound truth about the way God operates. There are things that He will do because He is faithful and He has decided to do them; however, who He uses and exactly how He works out all of His purposes and plans is negotiable. God is working out His plans, but to a large degree, "the how" depends upon the cooperation of people.

The Prophet Daniel understood this as well. Consider how Daniel was reading from the book of Jeremiah and learned that the Hebrew people were to be in captivity for 70 years (Dan. 9:2). As Daniel read Jeremiah's prophecy, he realized that the 70-year period of captivity was over and freedom was close at hand. However, Daniel did not sit around passively waiting for God to fulfill His promises. Instead, he went on a fast and sought God for the freedom and deliverance of the Hebrew people (Dan. 9:2-19). Daniel realized that he must cooperate with God for the fulfillment of what He had declared.

This principle works in our lives, too. In fact, James 4:2 tells us that we *"do not have because* [we] *do not ask."* This implies that there are many things which God is willing to do for us, but He will not do them until we ask Him. The fact is that our prayers actually do influence God and His actions.

This understanding gives awesome significance to our prayers and the actions we take.

It also offers the proper value, understanding, and honor to the covenant which God has made with us. As I explained earlier, a covenant is not a legal contract, but a commitment to a partner relationship. When we see how God allowed Abraham and Moses to influence His decisions, we are awed by the privilege God has offered to humankind through covenant. The same is true today. Through Jesus Christ, God's people have a covenant relationship with Him, and, therefore, a relationship of cooperation.

In contrast, the determinist view does not see the covenant as a partner relationship. According to that view, God already has made all of His decisions. Therefore, we truly cannot enter into the decision-making process with Him. The determinist sees the covenant as a one-way path wherein God gives us His promises and blessings, but no real mutual exchange can ever take place.

The Open View gives incredible significance to our

lives. We are not simply puppets walking out a predetermined plan; we have a free will and the possibility of
cooperating with God. Our prayers are important. God
listens. The Church is essential and it is actually being
raised to rule and reign with Jesus. We can work with
God to change the world and form the future.

Chapter 27
Our Lives and Vocations

Either God is **sovereign**, controlling all things, or He is sovereign, doing whatever He wants to do, whenever He wants. Let's consider this by applying it to the question: "How long will a person's lifetime be?"

Determinists believe that God decided before this world was created how long each human being would live. They like to quote David's words when he wrote:

> *Your eyes have seen my unformed substance;*
> *And in Your book were all written*
> *The days that were ordained for me,*
> *When as yet there was not one of them.*
>
> (Ps. 139:16)

Using this verse, determinists like to teach that the exact days of our lives are preset from the foundations of the world, and no one can change the date he or she is appointed to die.

I object to this use of Scripture. It is wrong to take a Bible verse in which David was talking about his own life and apply it to every human being who ever lived. God may have raised David for a specific purpose at a specific time in history in order to accomplish His predetermined plan. However, that gives us no basis to say that the life of every human being has been as tightly orchestrated.

Most people do play a significant role in determining

how long they live. What we eat, how we take care of our bodies, how we treat our parents (Eph. 6:2-3), how reckless we drive our automobiles, and what types of risks we take in life do influence how long we live on Earth. Of course, God can take a life whenever He chooses. However, within the limits set by God, each person plays a role in how long he or she will stay alive. Some people even die prematurely, that is, before God wanted them to die, as in the case of a suicide. Of course, God could have stopped their premature death—He has the authority and power to do so—but Scripture reveals that He has decided not to control things in this fashion. Because He is not controlling everything, people die, often outside of His plans and intended will.

This view allows us not to blame God when babies die at or before birth (an important point for our later discussion in Part VII). On the other hand, determinists say that from the foundations of the world, God appointed the day of birth and the day of death for every person. If determinists are going to be consistent, then they must apply this belief to adults, as well as babies. In contrast, the Open View does not have to blame God for the deaths of either.

This understanding keeps us from using harmful, trite phrases such as: "God took that child home," "It must have been his time," "It must be God's will," or "You will never die before your time."

God may have ordained certain people, such as David, Moses, Pharaoh, Jeremiah, and John the Baptist to live on Earth and fulfill a specific destiny during a set time period. However, there is no verse in the Bible which says every human being has an exact appointed day to be born and a day to die. To a great extent, our own lives are in our own hands.

Let's apply this truth to a person's life-calling and to what he or she will or will not accomplish while alive on Earth.

The deterministic Christian believes that God decided before this world was created what each person will accomplish while alive. To support their view, they often quote Bible passages which reveal God's control in certain individuals' decisions and actions. For example, God chose Jeremiah to be a prophet before Jeremiah was even born (Jer. 1:5). With similar sovereign authority, God chose to harden Pharaoh's heart in order to fulfill His purposes which He was working on behalf of the Hebrew people (Rom. 9:17-18). These, and a handful of other examples in the Bible, indicate that God can control the decisions of anyone He chooses at any time.

However, as a Christian with an Open View of God, I will point out that it is wrong to take a handful of examples and apply them to all people in all times. Even though God chose to use Jeremiah as a prophet, this does not necessarily mean that God is directing the career decisions of all six billion people on Earth today. God chose to take control of Pharaoh's decisions, but this does not mean that He was controlling each and every decision made by the two million Hebrew people.

Consider the words of Jesus when He spoke to His brethren about going to Judea:

> *"My time is not yet here, but your time is always opportune."*
>
> (John 7:6b)

From this we can conclude that the timing of our Lord's entrance into Judea was being orchestrated to fit into the overall plan of God. In contrast, the phrase, *"your time is always opportune"* implies that the timing for the others to enter Judea was not so significant nor tightly orchestrated.

Biblical revelation shows God dealing with different individuals in different ways. For example, our Lord intervened in the life of Saul, striking him with a flash of light (Acts 9:3-4). However, God does not strike every person with lightening. In the life of Jonah, we see God pursuing him until Jonah finally submitted to the will of God. However, God did not sovereignly seize the heart of Jonah, as He seized the heart of Pharaoh.

Most people seem to be wooed gently by the Holy Spirit. The love of God leads them to repentance; they respond to God in a step-by-step fashion. The Open View recognizes this and acknowledges varying amounts of God's influence, guidance, and control being exercised in the lives of different individuals. In fact, God's relationship with each and every human being is unique.

These varying relationships are especially evident when we contrast the lives of Christians and non-Christians. The steps of the righteous person are directed by the Lord, and the child of God can be led by the Holy Spirit. However, there is no assurance that God will guide the steps of the unrighteous person. In fact, the Open View sees non-Christians and sinners being allowed by God to go their own ways—except for times when God decides to intervene sovereignly and take charge, in order that He might fulfill some specific goal He has. The Open View also maintains that Christians can seek, through prayer, the intervention of God on behalf of others.

So, also, the gifts which God gives to Christians are not all predestined. First Corinthians 12:31 exhorts us to *"earnestly desire the greater gifts."* God responds to our desires. He is watching to see what will arise in our heart. We are told that the Spirit gives His gifts, *"distributing to each one individually just as He wills"* (I Cor. 12:11). The Open View sees this not as predestined gift-giving but the result of an interaction between God and individuals.

Another implication is in how an unmarried Christian may pursue finding a mate. The Christian holding a determinist view will look for that one person whom God has appointed as a partner. In contrast, Christians with an Open View will understand that there may be many different individuals out there whom they could marry and with whom they could be happy. The person they choose will become the right person by their commitment to them.

The Open View also recognizes that there are many options when it comes to choosing a career. God gives to individuals certain gifts and grace to accomplish specific tasks, but the person has much freedom in how to fulfill God's will. There must be cooperation between God and the individual. We must rise into the grace given to us. As the Apostle Paul wrote: *". . . I labor, striving according to His power, which mightily works within me"* (Col. 1:29).

We can and must work together with God.

Chapter 28
The Timing of the Second Coming

The Open View emphasizes human responsibility. To a great extent, we are in charge. God is steering things toward His ultimate goals, and He can control anything He wants to control. However, He has given us free will and much depends upon us.

Let's apply this to one more area—the timing of the Second Coming of our Lord Jesus.

The determinist sees all the related events as being set in time and everything working out exactly as pre-ordained by God. In contrast, the Open View sees God working out His plan in a cooperative fashion with people, and, therefore, many of the events of the future are still undetermined.

The Open View sees God watching over this world much as a farmer watches his fields. When the crop becomes ripe, then he goes out to bring in the harvest. In similar fashion, God is watching over humanity, and He is waiting until the fullness of the Gentiles comes in (Rom. 11:25). God is waiting and watching to see when humanity, and in particular the harvest and His Church are ready.

This Open View gives significance to the words of Peter:

> *The Lord is not slow about His promise, as some count slowness, but is patient toward*

*you, not wishing for any to perish but for all
to come to repentance.*

(II Pet. 3:9)

The context of this verse implies that our Lord is delaying
His return because He still wants to give more opportunities for people to come to Him. The concept of delay
contradicts the belief in a predetermined date.

So also does the declaration that our Lord is patient. If
He was timeless and presently filling all of time, patience
would be unnecessary and, in fact, irrelevant.

Further, the Open View of the return of our Lord gives
credence to the biblical evidence that we can influence
the date when Jesus returns. Peter exhorts us to live in
a way that will hasten the coming of the Lord (II Pet.
3:11-12). We are also encouraged to call on our Lord and
say, *"Come, Lord Jesus"* (Rev. 22:20). If the events and
dates were already determined, our prayers and activities to hasten the day would be in vain.

Of course, there may be a sequence of events that must
be fulfilled precisely as God ordains. We know that in the
past God has fulfilled certain promises on specific days
of a year. For example, the Day of Pentecost came on the
same day of the year that the Law was given to Moses.
Jesus was crucified during the time of Passover, which
shows amazing parallels between these two events. In
similar fashion, events of the Second Coming may correspond to days matching significant times mentioned
in the Old Testament. Future events may unfold in a
specific pattern; however, this says nothing about the
actual year in which those events will take place. The
time of fulfillment will come when God is ready.

For generations, we have had various Christian teachers trying to predict the date of the Second Coming, as if it were written in biblical code or buried in the Hebrew understanding of time. All such date-predictors have as an assumption that events are predestined, rather than yet to be declared by the Father in the fullness of times. The Open View sees the future as partially undetermined, and, therefore, it is foolish to predict dates. The date will be declared when the Father decides all things are ready. Yes, Jesus will return and every knee will bow to Him. However, the specifics and unfolding of the related events may not be determined yet. Furthermore, even if God has set the date, He still may change His mind and delay even longer, because He can sovereignly decide to allow more to be saved.

Part V
The Nature of
Humankind

Our understanding of God has profound implications on our understanding of the nature of humanity. In Part I, I briefly mentioned some implications of people being created in God's image, and of God having emotions and having both male and female attributes. In the following section, I address the implications of God's sovereignty; then I will focus on God the Creator, Lover, Covenant-Maker, and Father.

Chapter 29
Created in God's Image

If we reason that God is **sovereign,** in the sense that He controls and causes all things, then people are pawns, being moved about by the irresistible decisions and will of God.

The Classical Concept of God's Sovereignty and Its Implications on the Nature of Humanity:

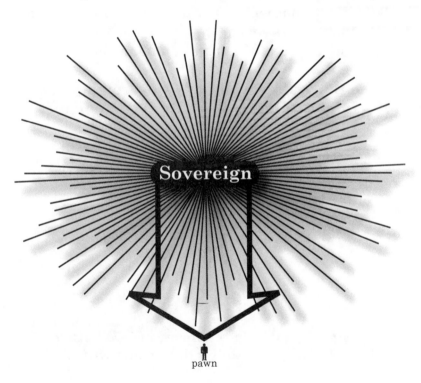

Sovereign

pawn

On the other hand, if sovereign means that God can do whatever He wants to do, then perhaps He sovereignly has decided to allow many things to move on their own. Perhaps Creation has some autonomy, with the ability to act independently of God's control. In particular, people have the ability to think, decide, and act on their own.

This concept of autonomy challenges us to think about the nature of humanity. How are we created? In what way are we created in the image of God? Perhaps we are created as God in the sense that we can initiate thoughts and actions. Maybe He created us for the purpose of relationship, and hence, we can have true relationship with Him. I dare say that this is the biblical revelation concerning the created nature of human beings.

The Biblical View of God's Sovereignty and Its Implications on the Nature of Humanity:

GOD

People Created in the Image of God with a Free Will and the Ability to Interact with God

With the Biblical View of God, we can say that God can control people's daily decisions if He so chooses, but in most cases He does not force His will on us. In fact, He works with us in a number of ways: He teaches us, guides us, inspires us, gives us His Word, and disciplines us. If God teaches us, then we can learn. If God gives us His Word, then we can hear it and obey or disobey. If God disciplines us with the goal of maturing us, then we can mature. Most importantly, we can make decisions; we can choose. We have a free will because we have been created in God's image.

Notice that I am describing the condition of all humanity—Christians and non-Christians. We are all created in God's image. Of course, sin can corrupt our relationship with God. Only through Jesus Christ can sinful humanity be reconciled to God and live in relationship with Him as children of God. However, the Apostle Paul explained that all people are the offspring of God (Acts 17:28-29). He Fathered all humanity.

Chapter 30
Capabilities of the Human Heart

We have identified two different definitions of the word sovereign: (1) God is **sovereign** in the sense that He is controlling all things; (2) God is sovereign in the sense that He can do whatever He wants to do whenever He wants to do it. The definition with which you agree will determine how you understand God and the nature of humanity.

It also determines how you interpret certain Scriptures. Consider I John 4:19:

We love, because He first loved us.

If you read this Scripture while holding to the Classical View of God, you will think of God with love emanating out of His nature as the sun emanates light. You will also see yourself reflecting God's love as the moon reflects the sun's light. Just as the moon is incapable of producing light, so also you will consciously and subconsciously think of yourself as incapable of loving without God being the source and cause of that love.

On the other hand, if you hold to the second definition of sovereignty and understand the implications which I have been discussing, you will read I John 4:19 and conclude something very different. It is true that we can only love God because He first loves us. However, you will see yourself as more than a sterile, impersonal "moon."

You are as a pile of wood that has caught fire. More than that, you are a human being capable of loving. Love is now coming out of your nature toward God.

If you hold and remain consistent to the Classical View of God, you may say that you love God, but by this statement you mean that God is loving Himself through you. In contrast, if you embrace the Biblical View of God and human nature, you can say from the depth of your heart, "I love God."

Evidence of this ability to love can be seen in the life of King David. Motivated by love for God David wanted to build a temple for Him (I Chron. 17:1-2). That good desire was not instilled in David by God. We know this because God forbade David to build the temple (I Chron. 17:3).

It is not only love which can come out of the heart of a human being, but we can take a closer look and discover other functions and capabilities of the human heart.

Think about how God can look into the heart of every person. Hebrews 4:13 tells us:

> *And there is no creature hidden from His sight,*
> *but all things are open and laid bare to the eyes*
> *of Him with whom we have to do.*

God can see into the very depth of our beings. Yet, we know from other verses that He continues watching to see what will proceed out of our hearts, and He tests us to see what is in our hearts (Gen. 22:12; Deut. 8:2; I Chron. 28:9). This leaves us with a question: If right now God is able to see everything which is in a person's heart, why does He keep watching (and testing) to see what will come out of the heart? The only way we can explain this is to say that new things can arise in a person's heart. Things which were not there one moment may arise later. This is the only reasonable conclusion. Furthermore, if God has to watch to see what will arise, then He must not be the source of all thoughts and desires.

Consider the evil in which the people of Judah engaged. God accused them of doing things *". . . which I had not commanded them nor had it entered My mind that they should do this abomination . . ."* (Jer. 32:35). This is tragic, yet profound. People came up with ideas and actions which God never had imagined. God was not the Unmoved Mover of these evils. In fact, He was surprised that people could contrive such evil.

People can initiate thoughts independently of God. This truth can only be embraced if we hold the Biblical View of God and humanity, rather than the Classical View.

People are creative. By saying this I am not implying that people can bring things into existence out of nothing. The Bible tells us that God created the heavens and Earth (Gen. 1:1), and all things came into being through Jesus (Col. 1:16). However, we can say that people are creative in the sense that they can initiate thoughts and desires. As a result, they can take that which God created and with their own imaginations use God's creation for good or evil.

This understanding of creative is more than the Classical View will allow. Teachers with a Classical View may say that people are creative, but by this they mean people can take what God created and rearrange it so that it appears differently. For example, they will agree that people can build homes, paint pictures, write books, and plan for the future. Of course, people are able to create in these fashions, but I am pointing out that the heart of a person can imagine things, that is, it can initiate ideas which result in good or evil (this will be a significant point for our discussion in Part VII).

Chapter 31
We Are Valuable

Christian teachers with a Classical View of God use many of the same terms when describing the nature of God and humanity that are used by Christians with a Biblical View. However, they mean something different. We have seen this with the words sovereign and creative. We also saw this with the word love, when I talked in the previous chapter about how people may love God. In a similar fashion, teachers from both perspectives will say that people are created in the image of God, yet they mean different things.

Building on the Classical View of God, teachers of Reformed theology say that people have *no intrinsic value.* Man is dust. However, according to Reformed theology, people do have *extrinsic value,* because God has **sovereignly** decided to value humanity. In other words, we have value because and only because God assigns value to us by choosing to value us.

In contrast, the Bible reveals that we do have intrinsic and extrinsic value. God created us in His image, and therefore, we are valuable by creation. Indeed, we are grand creatures. The Psalm-writer praises God, saying:

> *What is man that You take thought of him,*
> *And the son of man that You care for him?*
> *Yet You have made him a little lower than God,*
> *And You crown him with glory and majesty!*
>
> (Ps. 8:4-5)

Not only are people assigned dignity, but they are created as wonderful beings.

Of course, humanity has fallen, but the fact remains that God created us in His image. Even after the fall, God declared:

> *"Behold, the man has become like one of Us, knowing good and evil. . . ."*
>
> (Gen. 3:22)

God said we are *like* Him. Further, Genesis 5:1 tells us:

> *In the day when God created man, He made him in the likeness of God.*

The most fundamental aspect of our nature is that we are made in the image and likeness of God.

Teachers of Reformed theology have a difficult time accepting this at face value. They may say that people are created in the image of God, but in the next breath they will declare that we are but dust. They not only deny people's intrinsic value, but they exalt God to the point of being unlike us in all ways. It is common for Reformed theologians to declare that God is "wholly other," meaning God is completely of a different nature than humanity and any comparison is unimaginable. John Calvin wrote: "His essence, indeed, is incomprehensible, utterly transcending all human thought...."* With such views of

---

* John Calvin, *Institutes of the Christian Religion,* 2 vols., trans. Henry Beveridge (1845; reprint, Grand Rapids, Mich.: Eerdmans, 1964), 1:51 (1.5.1).

God and humanity, the Classical View envisions a gap of infinity between the nature of God and the nature of humanity.

This is similar to the Islamic view of God and humanity. Throughout history, Muslim philosophers have excelled in battles of logic, and the writings of Aristotle have played a central role in their thoughts. Hence, in the Islamic religion, God is seen as infinitely different than people. In fact, for Muslims the most a human can expect to attain is to become an obedient slave of God. It is impossible for a person to know God; at best a holy individual may know some of the ways of God. Furthermore, God could never take on human flesh, nor is it conceivable for God to put His infinite Spirit into a human being. The difference between God and humans is simply too great for any of these concepts to be possible.

Although the Classical Christian View of God does not go as far as the Islamic view, there are similarities because they are both founded on the ancient Greek Unmoved Mover. Within the Classical View, God is completely of another dimension, having nothing in common with the natural world. When God makes us His children, He is not really fathering us, but adopting creatures which are less than "microscopic worms" in comparison with Him.

Of course, the Biblical View recognizes areas in which God is *very different* than people. He always existed, having no beginning. His knowledge is infinite and ours is finite. In addition, God dwells in perfect light and glory, while we humans have all fallen short of His glory. In these and many other ways, God is much greater than we are, and yet, we are still created and exist in His image.

Classical View Versus the Biblical View:

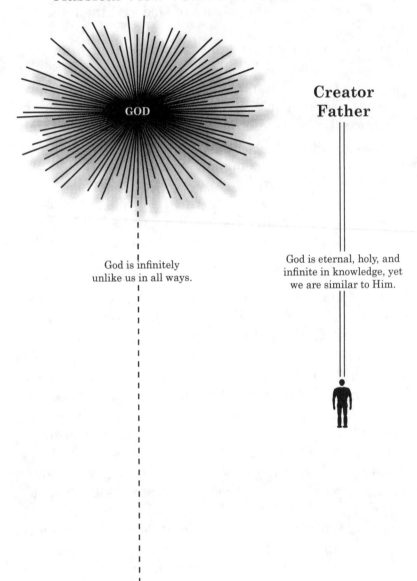

GOD

**Creator
Father**

God is infinitely
unlike us in all ways.

God is eternal, holy, and
infinite in knowledge, yet
we are similar to Him.

The implications of humanity being created in God's image are too vast to enumerate. After Noah's flood God warned:

"Whoever sheds man's blood,
By man his blood shall be shed,
For in the image of God
He made man."

(Gen. 9:6)

Because we are all created in God's image, it is a terrible thing to take the life of another human being. But our treatment of one another goes far beyond cautions about murder. The Judea/Christian ethic of the dignity of humanity lies at the foundation of all human rights. If all people are created in the image of God, then all people deserve to be treated with respect and care.

The Biblical View teaches that all people—Christians and non-Christians—are crowned with glory and majesty (Ps. 8:4-5). Therefore, everyone should value their neighbors as worth more than earthly treasures. A married person should cherish his or her spouse as an image-bearer of God. Children should be recognized as gifts of the Creator. All people must be respected and the overriding dynamic in relationships should be the desire to help everyone live and be treated as children of God.

Even more profound is how God Himself treats us with respect. Of course, He can do whatever He wants to do with His creatures, but He sees His own image in us, and therefore, treats us as grand creatures. This is most evident in His willingness to enter into relationship with us. God is willing to let us be His friends, His sons and daughters, His beloved.

Finally, we can note the honor given to humanity in God's willingness to put His Spirit into human vessels. As I mentioned earlier, the Islamic view of God disallows Muslims from comprehending how God could put His Spirit into a human being. The Classical View is not so harsh, but it is somewhat sterile, hindering Christians from fully grasping the intimacy implied in God's willingness to personally engage with us by His Spirit. The apostle Paul compares the Christian's spiritual union with God to sexual intimacy between a man and woman (I Cor. 6:16-17). Although this is a metaphor, the symbolism is revealing and profound. God has put His life in us. The impartation of His Spirit is not only a holy act, but it is intimate, giving, revealing, and personal. To bear God's Spirit is an honor beyond human comprehension.

Chapter 32
We Are Lovable

Because you and I are created in the image of God, we are lovable.

This truth is often missed with the Greek-originated, Classical View of God and its implications upon human nature. To the positive, we can note that Reformed theology allows Christians to be awed and overwhelmed by God's love. However, it sees God much as the sun, bathing all people with love, and that image makes no distinction between the people being bathed in that love. That love is too impersonal.

The God revealed in the Bible is not that way. He knows individuals. God knows our innermost thoughts. He loves us in our uniqueness.

Compare this with a parent with several children. A parent loves each child. A parent knows each child. Not only does a parent love each child because they are his or her children, but a parent loves each child as a unique individual.

Furthermore, to know and love a person is to embrace not only his or her good qualities, but also his or her weaknesses. For example, before our youngest child moved out on his own, he would come home from school and make a mess in the kitchen. My wife and I worked at trying to get him to clean up after himself, but we made little progress. At the same time, we have always loved our "mess-maker." It is a part of who he is.

God loves us in this fashion. This is not to make excuses for sins that we commit, but it is to realize that God knows our strengths and weaknesses, yet still loves us.

This point is so important that I need to emphasize it. The Greek-originated, Classical View of God leads us to believe that God loves us "in spite of our sins." That phrase, "in spite of our sins," can easily be misunderstood. With the Classical View of God, people tend to think of God as overlooking our sins so that He can love us. That image is not entirely accurate.

The Bible reveals a God who loves people—even sinners. Of course, God wants us to have victory over all sin, but He still loves sinners.

Compare this with a man who gives his life ministering to alcoholics. That minister loves alcoholics. He does not just love them in spite of their alcoholism. He loves them—period. He likes working with alcoholics. He has a heart for alcoholics. He loves people and wants to help them out of their problems.

Consider a mother who loves her mentally-disabled child. Of course, the mother wants what is best for her child. But her love is not only in spite of the mental disability. She loves her disabled child as he or she is.

God is that way. He loves people.

Think about a wife who faithfully and tenderly cares for her sick husband. Why does she do it? Because of love. Of course, she wants her husband to get well. But does she love her husband in spite of his sickness? Yes, but that statement does not say enough about her love. She doesn't have to block her husband's illness out of her mind in order to love him. She loves him in his sickness just as much as she would love him if he were healthy.

God loves sick people. God loves healthy people. He has a heart for alcoholics, drug users, the emotionally depressed, criminals, and the mentally insane. He loves people, not just in spite of their problems. He just loves people.

He loves us because we are created in His image. He loves us because we are unique. He loves us because we are creative, funny, industrious, social, artistic, and fraught with weaknesses and imperfections. Of course, He can get disappointed and even angry with us, but more importantly, He loves us as we are.

After God created Adam and Eve, He declared over His own Creation that it was *"very good."* If, indeed, we are created in His image, then we were created as wonderful creatures. In a sense, God thinks we are "cute." We are desirable. He loves us not only because He is love, but also because we are lovable.

Part VI
Implications of the
Sun-like Image

Over the course of the last 2,000 years of Church history, the philosophically-derived concept of an Immovable Mover evolved into a Sun-like Image of God. As we have seen, Christians subconsciously tend to see God as an invisible glowing Being radiating out His attributes. Even Christians who think of a God as an old man sitting up in heaven tend to think of Him radiating out His attributes filling the universe.

The Sun-like Image of God:

GOD

It is true that the Bible makes comparisons between God and light, but there is no justifiable reason for us to see that light as flowing out from a source. Consider how God created light on the first day of Creation, but He did not create the sun and stars until the fourth day. During the first three days, light simply existed without emanating from a source. With this as our comparison we can think of God's existence as light—not radiating out from a point—but simply existing throughout all.

It is impossible to accurately represent God's attributes in a diagram, but we need to see that God is not far away, radiating His attributes to where we are. He is right in front of us with all of His attributes. David wrote, *"If I ascend to heaven, You are there; If I make my bed in Sheol, behold You are there"* (Ps. 139:8). The Apostle Paul said that God is *"not far from each one of us"* (Acts 17:27).

God–Right in Front of You with All of His Attributes:

Implications of the Sun-like Image

To see how profoundly this distinction impacts Christian doctrine, we will look at God's love, His judgment, His will, and His goodness. Here in Part VI, you will see that if these attributes are removed from the image of a huge, glowing, sun-like force, Christian doctrine changes and our concept of God becomes more biblically accurate.

Chapter 33
Sun-like Love

Let's talk a little more about God's love. John wrote in his first letter, *"God is love"* (I John 4:8b). This declaration leads us to believe that love is not only an attribute of God, but His very substance and nature. If, however, we superimpose His love onto the Immovable Mover concept, we will envision love emanating out of God like light from the sun. We will also envision His love bathing all people evenly, indiscriminately, and unconditionally, regardless of who they are and what they do.

"Love" Superimposed upon the Sun-like Image of God:

LOVE

The sun-like image of God's love is impacted upon the minds of Western Christians through a teaching common in the Church today yet unfounded in Scripture. Many teachers like to point out that the Greek language from which our New Testament was interpreted uses three different words for love. These Greek words are *agape, phileo,* and *eros.* In distinguishing these words, teachers like to point out that *agape* is God's unconditional love, *phileo* refers to brotherly love, and *eros* is sexual or sensual love. Some Christian teachers today like to emphasize that God has "agape love" and they will point out that the Greek word used in I John 4:16 to tell us that God is love, is the word *agape.*

In defining agape love as God's unconditional love, Christians have to conclude that God has no conditions on the love He pours out. The average Christian who hears about this unconditional love of God develops a picture of God with love pouring out of His nature much as the sun baths everything in its path with light.

Now it is wonderful to reassure people that God loves them. It is commendable to tell people that God is willing to forgive them no matter what sins they have committed. Obviously, God's love is great.

However, let's ask the crucial question, "From where did this idea originate that *agape* means God's unconditional love?" Did this teaching come from the Bible? Did it originate with teachers who understand the Greek language? Or did it come from a teacher who simply was teaching what seemed to fit into his or her own theology? To answer this, let's look in a Bible Concordance to see where and how the Greek word, *agape,* is used in the Bible (*agape* is the noun; *agapeo* is the verb). In some

verses it refers to God's love; however, in other passages
it is used quite differently.

For example, consider the following verses in which the
word love has been translated from *agape* or *agapeo:*

> . . . *men loved the darkness rather than the
> light.* . . .
>
> (John 3:19)

> *for they loved the approval of men rather than
> the approval of God.*
>
> (John 12:43)

> *"Woe to you Pharisees! For you love the chief
> seats in the synagogues. . . ."*
>
> (Luke 11:42)

> . . . *for Demas, having loved this present world,
> has deserted me.* . . .
>
> (II Tim. 4:10)

> . . . *who love the wages of unrighteousness.*
>
> (II Pet. 2:15)

John, Luke, Paul, and Peter each used the Greek word
agape to speak of human love directed toward negative
things: darkness, the approval of men, the front seats
in the synagogues, this present world, and the wages of
unrighteousness. Luke 6:32 even tells us that it is natural
for sinners to have *agape* love for their own.

Do you see what this means? While many Christians
have been taught that the definition of *agape* is God's

unconditional love, that definition is inconsistent with its use in Scripture. That wrong definition is simply the natural interpretation if we superimpose the idea of love upon the sun-like image of God.

The truth is that the word *agape* was used in Jesus' day in everyday language when referring to love of all types. The most accurate translation we have of *agape* is not "unconditional love," but simply "love." (It is true, however, that *phileo* typically refers to brotherly or friendship love and *eros* is associated with sexual or sensual love.)

Why is this important? If we incorrectly define God's love as unconditional love, then we are saying that there are no grounds—no conditions—upon which God can decide to withdraw His love. We are in fact denying His sovereignty. That is a serious error. God is not an immovable force who evenly distributes His favor and love. He is not bound by a requirement to love. Love is still an act of His will.

Consider what God said about Jacob and Esau:

> *"Jacob I loved, but Esau I hated."*
>
> (Rom. 9:13b)

The Greek word interpreted as "hate" in this passages is *miseo*. Although thousands of Christians have tried to explain how this word does not really mean hate, there is no other appropriate interpretation. The word hate is placed in contrast to love. It means exactly what it says. God hated Esau.

The main point of this passage is not that God hates some individuals, but rather that He has the authority to do whatever He chooses to do. Paul went on in this passage quoting the words of God:

> *"I will have mercy on whom I have mercy, and I will have compassion on whom I have compassion."*
>
> (Rom. 9:15)

This statement is profound. God can and does choose. He is free—even in reference to His love. God will show compassion to whoever He so chooses to show compassion and He will love whomever He so chooses to love. He is sovereign.

Consider God's dislike for certain individuals:

> *And the one who loves violence His soul hates.*
>
> (Ps. 11:5b)

> *You hate all who do iniquity.*
>
> (Ps. 5:5)

Similarly we can read what God thinks about people who involve themselves in witchcraft:

> *"For whoever does these things is detestable to the Lord. . . ."*
>
> (Deut. 18:12)

There are times when God chooses to not love. Or He may cut certain individuals off from His love. He will not be mocked. There is a point at which He may turn His heart away from someone. Consider God's promise to treat Solomon differently than He dealt with Saul:

> . . . *but My lovingkindness shall not depart*
> *from him, as I took it away from Saul.* . . .
> (II Sam. 7:15)

God removed His lovingkindness from Saul. He warned
the Jews that He would deal with them in a similar
fashion:

> *Yet if in spite of this you do not obey Me, but*
> *act with hostility against Me, then I will act*
> *with wrathful hostility against you . . . for My*
> *soul shall abhor you.*
> (Lev. 26:27-30)

The word abhor has been translated from the Hebrew
word *gaal* which refers to the most harsh judgment including loathe and vilely cast away.

God can withdraw His love.

This is another truth incompatible with the Classical
View of God. Since that view insists that God is timeless,
He always would see the entire life-span of every person,
and therefore, there never would be a point in time in
which He would change His attitude toward a person.

Some people experience sincere discomfort in having
their concept of God's love challenged in this way. Often
it stems from a personal fear that perhaps God does not
love them. Allow me to sidestep for a moment to say that
this discussion need not make Christians insecure about
whether or not God loves them. Let me reassure you that
God fully loves those who have become His children. His

love is unconditional in the sense that God will overlook our sins and weaknesses. We can say that God has unconditional love for those who come to Him in faith.

Furthermore, God loves the world. However, we must understand His love for the world in light of the whole biblical revelation. John 3:16 tells us:

"For God so loved the world, that He gave His only begotten Son, that whoever believes in Him shall not perish, but have eternal life."

Obviously, God's love is great—beyond our understanding. However, John 3:16 is not a universal application of the unconditional love of God.

To see this, let me offer the example of Craig, a man who loves America so much that he would give away everything and even risk the life of his own son for America. Of course, this means that Craig has great love for America; however, it does not mean that he loves each and every person who lives in America.

In a comparative way, "God loves the world so much that He gave His Son." This emphasizes the greatness of His love; however, it does not mean that God loves every single individual who lives in the world. That is not what John 3:16 teaches. In fact, we can read 20 verses later (verse 36) that the *"wrath of God abides on"* those who do not believe in Jesus.

The point is that God has the authority within Himself to not love, and He occasionally exercises that authority. Love implies free will. It is easy to see this when we realize that God created us with a free will to love or not love. Just as humans are not robots, neither is God.

This truth is so significant that it is worth taking another chapter to further describe God's love.

Chapter 34
God Is Love

We must allow the revelation of God's love to stand
on its own, without the sun-like image at the foundation
of our thoughts.

**The Biblical View
Concerning God's Love:**

LOVE

Consisting of love does not necessitate that God loves
everything equally or indiscriminately. The application
of God's love is governed by His will. Where does God say,
"Do anything you want to Me, for as long as you like, and
I will continually love you—regardless"? Though often
stated or implied in many Christian circles, there is no
evidence of that in Scripture.

On the other hand, we would be equally ignorant to
argue that God's love for us is not long-suffering. God is
very patient with us. His long-suffering was evident in
His dealing with the Jews. It continues with us today.
Many of us have had the personal blessing of realizing that the love of God sought us out and hounded us
through our dark rabbit warrens of sin and destruction.
God's love often wins us over as we realize that it is not

going away, that we have not destroyed it. His strength is shown in His ability to love us and keep on loving us. For many of us, we realize that while we can hide from the sun, we cannot escape that light which shines around us and within us. We cannot escape this loving God.

His patience and long-suffering are central characteristics of His nature, yet long-suffering is not equivalent to forever suffering. He does have the sovereign ability to turn His heart away from an individual.

Imagining God's love as universal, constant, and non-discriminating may provide a measure of comfort, yet it does a huge disservice in that it violates both the nature of God's love and a fundamental human need. It is not enough to know that there is a source of boundless love in the universe which radiates to all humanity. That love does not satisfy our craving or need to be "picked out special." I want to be "picked out special." So do you. People long for personal love. They long to be loved for who they are—warts and blemishes, strengths and talents. They seek recognition on a personal and individual level.

Do not confuse this love with a love based on performance. The love for which we each long is the love based on intimacy. Two individuals love each other not because they are perfect, but because they have revealed themselves to each other. They have exposed themselves and they each still sense acceptance. They need not hide. They need not run away. They are okay.

People who cannot accept the personal love of God do so for a variety of reasons, mostly rooted in a low self-image. From an acute knowledge of their own sins or an exaggerated sense of their own unworthiness, they cannot accept that God would love them personally. Putting the love of God in personal terms is a threat to them. How can they measure up? How can they withstand the intimacy? How can they stand the exposure to a Holy God that such intimacy would bring? Easier and more comforting is the concept of a universal, all-loving, radiating God who bathes all in love, regardless of personal condition.

Yet that is not the revelation of God's love which is evident in the Bible. God doted on Jesus, saying, *"This is My beloved Son, in whom I am well-pleased"* (Matt. 3:17). Here we see God's love being expressed in terms of being pleased. Jesus hit the high mark. He pleased the Father.

Similarly, we can recognize God's personal feelings for Job as He talked with Satan.

> *"Have you considered My servant Job? For there is no one like him on the earth, a blameless and upright man, fearing God and turning away from evil."*
>
> (Job 1:8b)

God delighted in Job. He was proud of Job.

God experiences the emotions which a father experiences with his child.

The power of God's love—the reality of God's love—is not that it shines from heaven indiscriminately, but that it shines to each of us discriminatively. The power of God's love is not that it beams down to us universally, and the obedient or fortunate few manage to look up to catch a few of His rays. The power of God's love is that He knows me, sees me, can find me anywhere—and He likes me.

Chapter 35
Judgment and Atonement

Now let's consider the declaration, *"Our God is a consuming fire"* (Heb. 12:29). We generally associate this consuming fire with God's holiness and judgment. If we superimpose this aspect of God's nature upon the sun-like image, then we will envision fire, holiness, and judgment constantly emanating out of God as light out of the sun.

"Consuming Fire"
Superimposed upon the Sun-like Image of God:

CONSUMING
FIRE

This vision of God radiating out consuming fire has profound implications on our understanding of the atonement (the work accomplished through the death of Jesus). Please allow me to explain.

Envisioning God's judgment flowing toward all sin and unrighteousness, many of the great Christian leaders in history developed a serious misconception about the death of Jesus. The noted theologian Anselm (ca. 1033-1109) concluded that Jesus positioned Himself between us and the wrath of God. Like-thinking theologians reasoned that God *must* punish sin, and hence, Jesus took on the just wrath of God for humanity. The sun-like image of God leads us to think of the death of Jesus as a shield or a shock absorber between us and the just wrath of God which is directed toward all sin and unrighteousness.

**Misunderstanding the Atonement
(Jesus Taking on the Just Wrath of God):**

In reality, Jesus did not take on nor absorb the wrath of God. In His death, Jesus established with the Father a new covenant (Heb. 9:16-17). A central feature of that new covenant is that God forgave our sins (Heb. 8:12). If God forgave our sins, He did not have to take out His wrath on Jesus. Please allow me to explain this further.

Consider how Moses interceded for the Hebrew people when God became angry and almost destroyed them. Moses interceded and God changed His mind about doing harm to His people (Ex. 32:9-14). God did not take out His anger on Moses. Moses did not take on the wrath of God. Because of his relationship with God, Moses interceded and God listened, deciding not to punish the Hebrews.

In similar fashion, Jesus interceded for us. As a result, God changed His mind, subdued His anger, and forgave our sins.

Classical thinkers have a difficult time accepting this explanation of the atonement. They already have decided that the biblical record of God changing His mind is an anthropomorphism, not to be taken literally. Because they have assumed God is timeless, they cannot logically believe that God could change His mind about anything—especially judgment of sin. Hence, Moses did not change God's mind. According to their view of God, Jesus could not have changed God's mind either.

To see the Biblical View more clearly, consider the fact that Jesus was *"the propitiation for our sins"* (I John 2:2; 4:10; see also, Rom. 3:25; Heb. 2:17). A propitiation is neither a payment nor something which takes on the punishment for another person. It is a gift or action which appeases or eliminates the anger of someone. For an example of a propitiation from ancient times, think of a king with his army determined to destroy a city. The leaders of that city might send a great gift to the angry king in hopes of appeasing him. If the king receives the gift and his anger subsides, then the gift has served as a propitiation.

God sent His own Son to be the propitiation for our sins. His own Gift caused His anger to turn away from us so that we could be forgiven and be reconciled to Him.

This understanding of our sins being forgiven is key. You see, sins cannot be forgiven and at the same time paid for. It is one or the other, not both. Compare this to a person who owes a large sum of money to the local bank. If he cannot pay the debt, his brother may come and pay the debt for him. Once the debt is paid, the bank cannot say that it has forgiven the debt. No. Either the debt is forgiven or paid, but not both. Classical theism says that Jesus paid our debt. The Biblical View teaches that God forgave the debt.

In Hebrew 9:22 we are told, ". . . *without shedding of blood there is no forgiveness."* Classical thinkers like to take this verse and teach that the shedding of Jesus' blood paid the penalty for our sins. In reality, the context (Heb. 9:15-20) reveals that Jesus shed His blood not to pay for sins, but to establish a new covenant. In the new covenant our sins are forgiven.

To understand the workings of a covenant, consider God's dealings with the Hebrew people just before they came out of Egypt. He instructed them to kill a Passover lamb and sprinkle the blood of the lamb on the doorpost of their homes. The lamb did not take on the wrath of God, but the blood identified the people who had a covenant with God as the descendants of Abraham. The blood of the lamb marked the homes of those people so the death angel would not visit those homes. Jesus is our Passover Lamb. He shed His blood to establish a covenant for us.

God deals differently with people who are in covenant with Him than He does with those who are not in a covenant relationship. God forgives those who believe in Jesus, but *"the wrath of God abides"* on those who do not believe in Jesus (John 3:36).

The Biblical View
Concerning God and the Atonement:

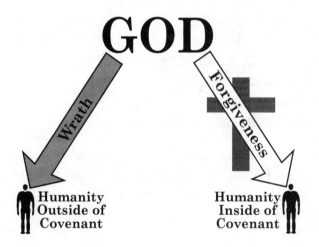

Jesus is not the wall between us and the wrath of God. He is the open door between us and a forgiving God. Furthermore, God is not a force with judgment flowing out of His nature toward all sin and unrighteousness. He can turn the judgment off. He can and will forgive sins. It is His nature to forgive.

Who Is God?

One of the most profound distinctions between these two views of the atonement becomes evident when we ask the question, "What killed Jesus?"

If we see the wrath of God flowing out of God as unyielding rays from the sun—or in other words, if we think of God as just in the sense that He must punish all sin—then we will conclude that the wrath of God killed Jesus as Jesus stood in our place before a God of judgment.

On the other hand, if we understand that God can forgive sins—truly forgive—then we will see that there is nothing inherent in God that needs to demand a penalty be paid for sin. The reason Jesus died is because He willingly took on our sins and the wages of sin is death (Rom. 6:23). A wage in this context refers to the natural consequence or outworking of sin. Therefore, our sins killed Jesus as He willingly received our sins upon Himself. Yes, our sins killed Jesus, not the wrath of God. * **

---

* Another problem with the idea that Jesus took on the wrath of God for the sins of humanity is that as a result there would be no more wrath to be poured out on judgment day upon those who reject Jesus. If Jesus took it all, then there would be no more! The only alternative to this is that Jesus only bore God's wrath on behalf of those whom He foreknew would receive Him. If we embrace that and we are logically consistent, then we are left with double predestination, that all people are predetestined by God to either heaven or hell. This is the reason that Christians consistent with Reformed Theology must believe in double predestination.

** For a more in-depth discussion of the atonement and related subjects, I recommend another book I have written, entitled, *Jesus Came Out of the Tomb...So Can You!*

Chapter 36
God and Prophecy

If we superimpose our understanding of God onto the sun-like image, then we will think of His Word proceeding from Him as rays from the sun.

**God's Spoken Word
Coming Forth from the Sun-like Image of God:**

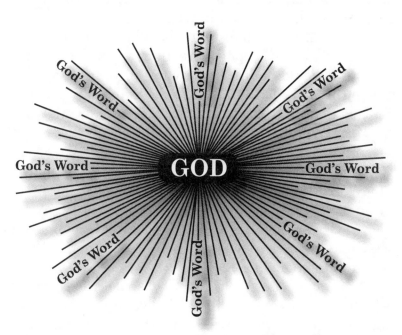

If God fills all of time, as the Classical View proposes, then He has already seen the future, and what He says must happen and nothing can change it. Even when God speaks His Word through a prophet, that which is declared must come true. With this at the foundation of one's view of God, a person is led to believe that when God speaks out His will, it is predestined to happen.

The Bible leads us to a different understanding of God's spoken Word. God can sovereignly send forth His Word in different ways. He can speak forth in a creative manner as He did when He said, "Let there be light" (Gen. 1;3). When God speaks with such authority, there is nothing that can stop His will from manifesting. On the other hand, God can send forth His Word in a less authoritative manner, so that its fulfillment is conditional and may require the cooperation of people.

For example, Daniel read the Words of God which came through the Prophet Jeremiah, and he learned that the Jews would be in captivity for 70 years (Dan. 9:2). When Daniel learned this, he immediately began to pray for God to fulfill His promise (Dan. 9:3-19). Daniel knew that the Word spoken through the Prophet Jeremiah was not predestined to happen, but someone needed to intercede and cooperate with God for the fulfillment of His Word.

So it is with many prophecies. They may be the expression of God's will—His heart, His desire, His plan—but they may require someone to believe the spoken Words before they come into reality.

There are some Words of God spoken by prophets which never become fulfilled. For example, Jonah went throughout Nineveh proclaiming that God was about to destroy the city (Jon. 3:4). In response, the people repented and *"God relented concerning the calamity which He had declared He would bring upon them"* (Jon. 3:10). The Word of God spoken through the prophet was not fulfilled.

This truth is incompatible with the Classical View of God. Adherents must say that it is impossible for God to change His mind and the account in Jonah is simply a figure of speech.

Yet, God speaks through Jeremiah that He often deals with people in such a conditional fashion.

> *"At one moment I might speak concerning a nation or concerning a kingdom to uproot, to pull down, or to destroy it; if that nation against which I have spoken turns from its evil, I will relent concerning the calamity I planned to bring on it."*

(Jer. 18:7-8)

The idea that God decides something, speaks out His decision, and then changes His mind, is in direct conflict with the Classical View of God. Yet, this is what the Bible shows us to be true.

An excellent example of this is from the life of Hezekiah. When Hezekiah became mortally sick, Isaiah the prophet said to him:

> *"Thus says the Lord, the God of Israel, 'Set your house in order, for you shall die and not live.' "*

(II Kings 19:20b)

When Hezekiah heard this Word, he prayed and God heard his prayer, healed him, and added 15 years to His life. In this case we see that the Word of the Lord which

183

first came through Isaiah did not come true, because God changed His mind.

There is a passage in Isaiah in which God tells us that He sends forth His Word, and it will not return void (Is. 55:11). Someone who believes the Classical View may take this verse and teach that God's Word always accomplishes what it is sent out to do, but that would be a misunderstanding of this verse. In the context, God was speaking through Isaiah about what He had decided to do with Israel at a specific time in history. It was a case in which God had made an unchangeable promise. In that case, God declared His Word was not going to return void. Indeed, God can speak out His Word whenever He wants in such an authoritative fashion. However, it is wrong to take this one verse and apply it to every situation in which God speaks. There are many times when He speaks and sends out His Word in a conditional manner.

Jesus even told a parable how the Word of God is similar to seeds cast into the soil. Some of those seeds land in good soil, take root, and produce. Other seeds land along the road, or in the rocky soil, or in the thorns, and never produce what they were sent out to do (Matt. 13:3-23). God does send out His Word, but the receptivity of people often determines whether or not that Word bears fruit.

God's Word does not flow out of His nature as rays from the sun. He can sovereignly send forth His Word with various degrees of authority. After all, He is God and He can do whatever He wants to do.

Chapter 37
Praying According to God's Will

We already have seen implications of our concept of God upon prayer. If God actually listens to us, then we can do more than move mountains—we can move God. If we truly have a covenant with God, then He will allow us to speak into certain situations. If we truly have a cooperative relationship with God, then we can form the future with Him.

Another implication has to do with our manner of praying. To see this, consider one of the biblical promises concerning prayer:

> . . . *if we ask anything according to His will,*
> *He hears us.*
>
> (I John 5:14)

This verse tells us that we must ask *"according to His will."* How we understand this requirement depends upon our concept of God. Allow me to explain.

If we have a sun-like image of God at the foundation of our understanding, then we will think of God's will as emanating out of Him as rays of light from the sun. We will tend to think of His will flowing out of Him as forces forming and maintaining the universe.

With this image in mind, Christians who pray will attempt to align their prayers with the will of God. Since the Bible tells us that we must pray *"according to His will,"* Christians will try to figure out what God's will is, and then formulate their prayers to match what He already desires to do.

A Person Praying to God Whose Will Is Superimposed upon the Sun-like Image:

On the other hand, if we remove the sun-like image from the foundation of our thinking of God, then we will have a different understanding of prayer. Consider the promise of Jesus in the Gospel of John:

> *". . . ask whatever you wish, and it will be done for you."*

> (John 15:7)

Here we are assured that we can ask whatever "we wish." These words do not point to God's will, but to our own will. I do not mean to imply that we can ask any carnal desire and God will respond. The context of this verse tells us that we must be abiding in Jesus. However, God is a Father who wants to hear "our desires." He wants us to be free enough and confident enough with Him that we will approach Him with our concerns.

If, indeed, we can ask according to our wishes and our desires, what does it mean that we must pray "according to God's will"? Do we have to bring our will in line with God's before He will answer? If so, why even pray, since He is going to do His will anyway?

Consider a different understanding of the phrase, "pray according to His will." Think of it as praying "as God wills." Pray in the manner in which God wants us to pray. If we pray in the manner in which He wants us to pray, then He will answer. With this understanding, our efforts in prayer will not be to try to make our prayers match His will, but to pray our own desires and to pray as God wants us to pray our desires.

And how does God want us to pray? He wants us to have contact with Him. He wants us to dialogue as a son to a Father. God wants us to reason with Him, as Abraham did (Gen. 18:22-33). He wants us to speak face to face with Him, as Moses did. He wants us to call Him Father (Matt. 6:9). God wants us to know Him. He wants us to engage with Him.

This understanding of prayer corresponds to the biblical exhortations to pray in the name of Jesus. Our Lord said:

187

> *"Truly, truly, I say to you, if you ask the Father for anything in My name, He will give it to you."*
>
> (John 16:23)

Again, this passage is not exhorting us to find out what God's will is and then to make our prayers match His will. No. He tells us to pray "anything" and if we pray in His name, God will answer. The focus is not on what we pray for but on how we pray.

To pray in the name of Jesus is to pray as if we were asking on His behalf, in His stead. As we abide in Jesus, we can ask anything and God will answer.

Of course, God's answers do not always come as we expect. If a child asks his father for financial help, his father is not always going to hand him a financial gift; a wise father may choose to teach that child how to work. A businesswoman who asks for help in her business can expect God to answer as a Covenant-Partner, giving counsel and guiding her through daily decisions. If a Christian sees a poor beggar on the road and he asks God to help that individual, God may answer by saying, "You help him." Of course, there will be times when God sovereignly intervenes and there will be times when God acts supernaturally, however, the primary way God wants to answer prayers is by working with us.

Chapter 38
Our Image of God
And Our Ethics

Our image of God profoundly influences what we believe is right or wrong. In this book I cannot address all the numerous ethical issues facing us today, but I will discuss one area to demonstrate how our image of God determines our ethics.

As we explained, Classical-minded Christians tend to think of God's will as emanating out of Him as rays from the sun. Since God is the ultimate reference point for what is right and what is wrong, the believer will try to determine what God's will is and then submit to that will. Anything contrary to that is wrong.

With this image of God, let's consider how a Christian couple may decide how many children they will have. In this discussion, I am not addressing the various forms of birth control which are available today. That topic would take another book to discuss. The only ethical question to which I want to speak here is the basis upon which a Christian couple decides how many children they will have.

If they envision God as timeless, immutable, **sovereign**, and in control of all things, then they will question whether or not they should even plan the number of children they should have. They will tend to think that God created all things for a specific purpose, and therefore, humanity should not interfere with that purpose. To interfere is, in a sense, to "play God." Classical-minded believers will tend to think that some element of chance should be left in the whole reproductive process so that they can truly leave God's decisions to God.

Although this is a logical way of thinking for the Classical-minded Christian, most people do not live logically consistent with their own beliefs. They wrestle with the implications but they rationalize what they want to do anyway. The Roman Catholic Church is fairly consistent with and true to its Augustinian theological roots, and therefore, has strong teachings about interfering with the natural reproductive processes. Most Classical-minded Protestants part from their theological roots on this ethical issue, but they still wrestle with questions and inner turmoil.

In order to cleanly break away from the reproductive ethics consistent with the Classical View of God, we first need to disrupt the Classical idea that God **sovereignly** determines when every individual will be born. We already discussed (chapter 27) how Classical thinkers err when they take Psalm 139:16 and from this verse conclude that every person's lifespan is predetermined. Biblical revelation leads us to believe that God does not control every person's life in such a fashion.

Of course, God can predestine any person's birth, however, the Bible reveals to us that there are some people who are born whom God never wanted to be born. For example, in Noah's day *". . . the sons of God came in to the daughters of men, and they bore children to them"* (Gen. 6:4). Different Bible scholars understand this in various ways, but it is clear that God did not approve of what was going on. Consider also how Tamar bore twins after she disguised herself as a harlot and had relations with

Judah, her father-in-law (Gen. 38). Did God arrange, predestine, or even want this sexual encounter, and hence, these children to be born? The Bible testimony makes it clear that He did not.

This can be very unsettling for Christians who have been raised in Classical theology. To them, it is unthinkable that God has not predestined every person who will be born. Yet, the biblical testimony is clear. There are some people who are born whom God did not predetermine to be born.

Once we abandon the idea that God is in total control of who will be born and when they will be born, then we can embrace the responsibility that people have in reproductive choices. Of course, God is sovereign, and therefore, He can intervene, cause a woman to be barren, or make another fertile, but much also depends upon our decisions. If we accept our responsibility in this, we will rise to make responsible, wise decisions. The personal desires of the parents also factor into the decision: How many children do they want?

Christians with a Biblical View will not only depend upon their own wisdom and desires. A proper understanding of covenant makes Christians aware of the relationship they have with God as a Covenant-Partner. Recognizing this, Christians will pray, ask God's guidance, and allow God to enter into the decision-making process. According to the Biblical View of God and humanity, what is ethically right is for the Christian couple to make their best judgment possible, depending upon God to guide them concerning how many children they should have; to do otherwise would be ethically wrong.

In similar fashion, all ethical issues should be

addressed with a Biblical View of God and humanity. Christians who are consistent with the Classical View of God will not realize the extent of free will given to humanity, and therefore, they will tend to err on the side of irresponsibility. They will not realize the God-given honor they bear and the responsibility entrusted to them to make decisions which govern this world. They will misunderstand the significance of the covenant relationship with God, and thinking that they are aligning themselves with God, may be making decisions apart from Him; that is, apart from the covenant relationship in which God desires to work with humanity.

Again, let me say that this is not a book on ethics, however, our concept of God profoundly influences our ethics, so we have another reason to carefully develop an accurate view of God.

Chapter 39
God Is Good

God is good, however, we will misunderstand His nature if we superimpose His goodness upon the sun-like image.

God's Goodness
Superimposed upon the Sun-like Image of God:

If we see God's goodness as always flowing out of His nature, then we are denying His sovereign ability to give favor to some individuals or to turn off the flow of goodness to others. Of course, God allows His goodness to benefit both the righteous and the unrighteous (Matt.

5:45), however, He does not treat all people the same. As we saw in Part I (chapters 6 and 7), God gives favor to some and not to others. His favor has nothing to do with ethnicity nor status in life, but He does show His kindness differently to different individuals. Therefore, we must state that God is good and allow that attribute to stand on its own, without the sun-like image at the foundation.

The Biblical View
Concerning God's Goodness:

GOOD

Some Christians have a difficult time separating the goodness of God from the sun-like image. They reason that if God is good, then He must have goodness constantly flowing out of Him. Yet, if God turned off the flow of goodness, He would still be good. In fact, God can do whatever He wants to do and He still is good, because He defines what good is.

This realization has profound implications on our understanding of suffering, pain, and the origin of death and evil, as we will see in Part VII.

Before we delve into those subjects, allow me to summarize this section by saying, "God is more as Jesus than He is as the sun." God is good, as Jesus is good. God works out His will in the earth as Jesus works out His will in the earth. God is love, as Jesus is love.

Many Christians consciously and subconsciously think of God the Father as the sun, while thinking of Jesus in human form with flesh and bones. The gap, therefore, between their understanding of the Father and their understanding of the Son is huge, even infinite.

In reality, Jesus is the exact representation of the Father (Heb. 1:3). Jesus told His disciples that if they had seen Him they had seen the Father (John 14:9). As Jesus felt compassion, the Father felt compassion. As Jesus died on the cross, God was in Christ reconciling the world to Himself (II Cor. 5:19). Of course, we know that Jesus emptied Himself as He became flesh (Phil. 2:7). We have not seen Him in all of His glory. Yet, He is as the Father. We cannot go wrong by worshipping Him.

Part VII
Death, Evil,
And Suffering

The historic test of a philosopher's logical integrity is revealed when answering the question, "If God is good, why is there so much suffering and pain?"

Since the Classical View of God teaches that God is in control, proponents must spend much time and energy wrestling with this issue. If He is truly in control, then He determines and orchestrates the pain and suffering you and I experience. If He predestined all things from the foundations of the world, then ultimately He is the cause of all things. If God is the Immovable Mover of all things, then He is responsible.

If we embrace the Biblical View, that is if we remove the sun-like image from the foundation of our concept of God, then we will deduce a different understanding about the origin of death, evil, and suffering.

Chapter 40
The Nature of Creation

If we hold to the sun-like image of God and we perceive God as good, then we will envision all of Creation as originally designed by God as good. Hence, Classically-trained Christians typically envision the Garden of Eden as a place where no death, suffering, nor pain existed. Bushes had no thorns and no animals killed other animals. Everything God created was good in the sense that it was peaceful, orderly, and non-harmful.

Good Flowing from a Good Creator:

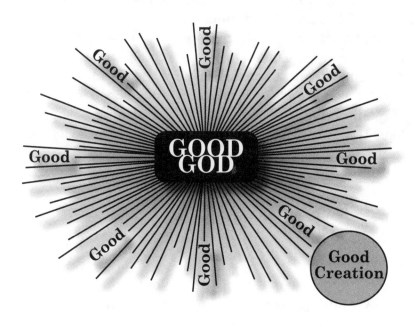

That concept is not entirely accurate according to the biblical account. To see this, note that God told Adam and Eve to take dominion over Earth (Gen. 1:28). Then He placed Adam and Eve in the Garden to tend it. By this we can conclude that Creation was designed with a need for maintenance and cultivation by humans. Plants did not grow in straight rows by themselves. Weeds grew in the garden. Adam and Eve were expected to work six days each week to manage the Garden.

This is fascinating because it implies that God created things in a needy condition. Creation was good, but not good in the sense of being complete in itself. Certainly, it was in God's plan to design the world in this fashion, but the deeper point is that out of God's nature came forth things which needed domination, in the sense of stewardship and caretaking.

Next, consider the thorns which grow on some plants. It is common for Classical thinkers to say that there were no plants which grew thorns before the fall of Adam and Eve. That concept, however, is only developed as a result of reading the Bible through the Classical philosophical lens. It is true that after Adam and Eve sinned, God said to them:

> *"Cursed is the ground because of you;*
> *In toil you will eat of it*
> *All of the days of your life.*
> *Both thorns and thistles it shall grow for you. . . . "*
> (Gen. 3:17-18)

Indeed, cultivation became more difficult and strenuous. However, there is no verse which indicates that thorns and thistles did not already exist before the fall. What is implied in Genesis 3 is simply that humanity would lose some authority over nature, and hence, thorns and thistles—which may have already existed—would grow where they were not wanted. Similarly with weeds: they already existed, but they may have gotten worse and more out of control since Adam and Eve sinned. The point to consider is that God did not create this world as a warm and fuzzy environment without thorns or weeds.

Examine the words of Paul as he stood before the Greek philosophers and taught about God and Creation:

> "... who made the world and all things in it ... and He made from one man every nation of mankind ... that they would seek God, if perhaps they might grope for Him and find Him. ..."
>
> (Acts 17:24-27)

The primary reason God created this world was to bring into existence a people who would seek Him—even grope for Him.

To accomplish this, God placed us in a world in which we need help. It is a big world, an unfinished world, a world that needs to be managed. Most importantly, we cannot be successful here without Him. This world is good in the sense that it needs us and God working together to manage it.

Allow me to offer a comparison from my own life. I built a woodworking shop in which my youngest son and I enjoy building things. Some of the tools are dangerous. It is easy to cut oneself on a power saw; and although there are dangers, my shop is not evil. It is good. It is good in the sense that my son and I can build things there. Even more wonderful is the fact that he comes to me occasionally and asks my advice. I like that. The shop is a place where we can build a relationship.

God created the world that way. There are difficult and even dangerous things which cause us to seek His advice, and, at times, grope for Him. There are also beautiful things which reveal His glory. The rain which causes crops to grow can flood homes and kill people. The wind can blow and carry seeds to fertile ground, but it can also dislodge a bird's nest from a tree, resulting in the death of young chicks. The ocean shouts of the magnificence of our Creator, yet, it also beats against the cliff's base, eventually causing it to crumble, burying all in its path.

The world is not a big pillow upon which people are to spend their lives sleeping and casually eating. It needs to be managed. People need to work. They can only be successful with God's assistance. They need God. This world is good in the sense that it is the perfect environment to fulfill God's purpose—to lead people into a relationship with Him.

Chapter 41
The Origin of Death

Since Classically-trained Christians only envision good flowing out of a good God, they have a difficult time conceiving of death in Creation before the fall of Adam and Eve. They typically explain that death (and all other evils) are the result of Satan corrupting the good things that God created. Then they say that death found access into this world as Adam sinned and submitted to Satan's will. Romans 5:12 is a verse often used to support this viewpoint:

> *Therefore, just as through one man sin entered into the world, and death through sin, and so death spread to all men, because all sinned....*

With this verse a picture is drawn in the minds of listeners that God created life, Satan corrupted it, and then Adam allowed death to sweep into the Garden of Eden and into the whole world.

In reality, God created life and death in the beginning. Furthermore, He instilled the cycles of life and death in nature itself.

To see that death was in existence before the sin of humanity, consider the original conditions of the Garden of Eden. In the very beginning, God instructed Adam and Eve to eat of every plant yielding seed and fruit (except, of course, from the tree of the knowledge of good and evil; Gen. 1:29). Every time a plant is eaten it dies. The human digestive system breaks down every living cell before absorbing it. So, in God's original design, we recognize one form of death in existence prior to the sin of Adam.

It is not only plants which experienced death in the Garden of Eden. Consider the fact that plants are covered with bacteria and other microscopic organisms. Thousands, even millions of these organisms are consumed each time a plant is eaten. Most of those microscopic organisms die within the human digestive system.

Think about the fur, hair, and feathers that grow from the skin on certain animals. Did you know that the root of every hair and feather is made of living cells? Those cells die as they emerge from the skin. If there were no death in Creation, then every hair and feather that was ever lost would still be lying on the ground alive. That is not how God designed this world. Life and death were a part of His original design.

Next, consider large animals. Picture an elephant walking through a forest. Is it possible for an elephant to walk more than a mile without stepping on and crushing a few insects? I doubt it.

Consider rabbits and how fast they reproduce. If you allow rabbits to reproduce unhindered, with none of them dying, every square foot of Earth's surface will be covered by a living rabbit in less than 100 years.

Beetles are even more prolific. If they reproduce unhindered for more than 50 years, Earth will be covered with a layer of beetles several feet deep.

How did God originally create this world? Plants and animals were not created to be immortal. Death was in His original design. This does not include the death of humans, which I will explain in just a moment, but, indeed, life and death were instilled in the nature of plants and animals from the beginning.

For proof of this, consider the words of God to Job. God declared that He created the lion to hunt and kill her prey (Job 38:39), the wild ox to be untameable (Job 39:5-12), the ostrich to treat her young cruelly (Job 39:16), the eagle to spy out food from afar while the young suck blood (Job 39:26-30), and Leviathan with teeth that terrify (Job 41:14). Make no mistake about this truth: God created animals which kill and eat one another.

Death is not necessarily an evil thing. It is a part of nature.

How did death come upon humanity?

Humans originally were given authority over everything upon Earth—including authority over death. But God declared to Adam and Eve that in the day they ate from the forbidden tree they would die (Gen. 2:17). When they disobeyed God, humanity became subjected to death. Consider again Romans 5:12:

> . . . *so death spread to all men, because all sinned.* . . .

This verse says nothing about death coming into the plant and animal kingdom. Indeed, death was an original element of natural Creation. What occurred when Adam sinned is that humanity lost authority over death. Hence, the power of death overcame and spread to all of humanity.

Chapter 42
The Origin of Evil

The Bible reveals to us that evil is in the world as a result of Satan and his demons. This is a huge subject and many books have been written about it, but I will not be expounding on the nature and activities of Satan or his demons. Both the Classical and Biblical Views acknowledge the work of evil spirit beings, but the Biblical View sees an additional source of evil.

Jesus talked about evil coming from the hearts of human beings:

> *"For from within, out of the heart of men, proceed the evil thoughts, fornications, thefts, murders, adulteries, deeds of coveting and wickedness, as well as deceit, sensuality, envy, slander, pride and foolishness. All these evil things proceed from within. . . ."*
>
> (Mark 7:21-23)

Yes, evil can come from within—from within the hearts of people.

This explanation is not compatible with the Classical understanding, because that leads us to believe that God is **sovereign** in the sense that He is the only Initiator. Augustine would say that God pushed all things into existence, and this includes Satan who later rebelled to God. So, according to the Classical View, God is not the direct cause of evil, but He is indirectly the cause because He is the Immovable Mover who pushed all things into existence.

What does the Bible teach? As I mentioned at the beginning of this chapter, Satan and his demons are responsible for much of the evil in the world, but earlier we looked at Jeremiah 32, where God accused the Jewish people of doing things "... *which I had not commanded them nor had it entered My mind that they should do this abomination* ..." (Jer. 32:35; see also 7:31; 19:5). The implication is that this evil came into existence out of the imaginations of people's hearts.

The Apostle James confirms that this happens.

> *But each one is tempted when he is carried away and enticed by his own lust. Then when lust has conceived, it gives birth to sin; and when sin is accomplished, it brings forth death.*
>
> (Jas. 1:14-15)

The context of this passage is a discussion of the origin of evil. James is reassuring us that good things come from God (1:13, 16-17). In contrast, evil is the result of people being carried away by their own lusts. Of course, Satan can be involved in tempting people, but in this context James makes no mention of Satan nor his demons. He explains that people's lusts give birth to sin.

Consider again Paul's words in Roman 5:12:

> *Therefore, just as through one man sin entered into the world.* . . .

If we read this verse with a Classical mind, we will

most likely envision Adam as *a conduit* for evil which originates with Satan and flows into this world. That is a reasonable explanation. However, if we believe that people are able to initiate thoughts and desires, then evil may have also originated in and came out of the heart of Adam.

Adam's descendants are also created in the image of God, and hence, they are able to initiate thoughts. Therefore, people are capable of bringing forth evil from their own hearts. Hence, all humans share responsibility for the evil presently in this world.

Chapter 43
Suffering and Pain Happen

Because evil exists, there is a tremendous amount of suffering and pain in this world. War, murder, and hate are the result of people's wickedness. Humans reap the consequences of their own actions. Satan and his demons also are active, seeking people to hurt and devour.

However, these are not the only sources of suffering and pain.

Some forms of pain are "natural." For example, God created people with nerves permeating their outer skin tissues. Adam and Eve must have had nerves in the bottoms of their feet, helping them to avoid stepping on sharp rocks. Similarly, their eyes must have had nerves sensitive to pain, lest they poke their eyes out on a tree branch. God created people that way. Of course, pain may have gotten worse as a result of the sin of humanity, but it is reasonable to think that God originally created people with the ability to feel physical pain.

Some suffering and pain is natural, in the sense that it results from the natural processes which God set in motion at Creation.

Consider how the earth has a hot molten center which sometimes builds up tremendous pressures, even enough to cause a volcano to erupt. God created Earth this way. Plants, animals, and even people die in volcanic eruptions. I propose to you that some of those people die by chance rather than by God's predetermined plan. We live in a world where chance is real and risks are unavoidable.

According to the Classical View there is no such thing as chance. If God is the Timeless Immovable Mover who has predestined all things, then chance is nonexistent.

On the other hand, if God is sovereign in the sense that He does whatever He wants to do, whenever He wants to do it, then He may be allowing many things in this world to proceed according to natural processes.

I believe many happenings in Creation occur by natural processes. Seeds are carried along and dispersed by the wind. Some seeds burst forth from pods. Some of those seeds land in good soil and others in rocky soil. Some are eaten by birds and some take root and live. Indeed, Creation reveals a tremendous amount of randomness and chance.

Of course, there are natural laws governing all things—even the way in which the wind carries a seed and a volcano erupts—but here I am referring to things which happen by chance, in the sense that they occur without God's control. Of course, God can control whatever He wants to control, but He has sovereignly decided not to control everything.

Consider what happened to the Philistines when they stole the ark of God from Israel and took it into a Philistine city (I Sam. 4-5). The Philistines experienced an outbreak of tumors and great confusion, so the leaders of the city placed the ark on a cart pulled by two cows. Then they watched the cart to see if it would be taken directly back to the Israelites or if it would be pulled randomly into the wilderness. The leaders knew that if God did not take the cart back, then "... *it was not His hand that struck us; it happened to us by chance"* (I Sam. 6:9). They understood that some things happen by God's hand and some things happen by chance.

King Solomon explained how all people are subject to chance:

> *I again saw under the sun that the race is not to the swift and the battle is not to the warriors, and neither is bread to the wise nor wealth to the discerning nor favor to men of ability; for time and chance overtake them all.*
>
> (Eccl. 9:11)

Chance is real.

A friend of mine was crushed by a huge branch which broke free from a tree overhead. He was left handicapped and in pain for years. I don't believe he deserved that, and I don't believe it was punishment for sin. It did not happen because God made the branch break, but because branches sometimes get old and gravity pulls them to the ground.

Of course, God could have prevented that, or any other tragedy, from happening. He can do whatever He wants to do. However, He is not obligated to. He is sovereign. He has chosen not to control everything.

Chapter 44
God Can
Cause Suffering

Suffering and pain are not necessarily evil. In fact, some suffering and pain may be caused by God. To see this, let's look in the Bible to see how God acts toward His Creation and how His actions, at times, may cause suffering and pain.

In Genesis 5:29, we read about *"the ground which the Lord has cursed."* What is eye-opening is the fact that a curse came out of God. He cursed Earth.

Some Christians cannot envision anything negative coming out of God's nature. So deeply rooted in their minds is the sun-like image of God that they can only think of "warm fuzzy things" flowing out of a good God.

I will reaffirm repeatedly the truth that God is good; however, we need to reconsider what good is. Furthermore, we need to identify what can and does come forth from God.

Consider the flood in Noah's day. Tens of thousands, if not millions, of people were killed. Also the plant and animal life, along with much of the environment, were destroyed. God did this.

It is easy to justify in our minds the destruction that happened in Noah's day because we recognize that God is God. It is His Creation and whatever He does is justifiable. However, what we are considering here is the nature of the actions of God. It is incorrect to think of only "nice things" flowing out of God. That is not who He is.

I am not suggesting that God is bad. I am challenging the sun-like image of God. I am endeavoring to explain that the benevolent-only concept does not match the biblical revelation. It is not true that pain and suffering can only be the result of an evil intermediary between God and Creation. There are many Scriptural examples where pain and suffering are the direct result of God's involvement with Creation. For example, God promised Abraham, "... *the one who curses you I will curse*..." (Gen. 12:3). Yes, God has promised to "*curse*" people who curse Abraham.

Lest we think Noah's flood is an isolated example, scan through the book of Genesis and note other examples of God's actions which cannot be described as peaceful, gentle, or kind. For example, God promised Abraham, "... *the one who curses you I will curse*..." (Gen. 12:3). Yes, God has promised to "*curse*" people who curse Abraham.

Listed below are other eye-opening passages from Genesis that support this reality.

> *But the Lord struck Pharaoh and his house with great plagues.* . . .
>
> (Gen. 12:17)

> *Then the Lord rained on Sodom and Gomorrah brimstone and fire from the Lord out of heaven, and He overthrew those cities.* . . .
>
> (Gen. 19:24-25)

> *For the Lord had closed fast all the wombs of the household of Abimelech.* . . .
>
> (Gen. 20:18)

> . . . *God has shown to Pharaoh what He is*

*about to do . . . and the famine will ravage the
land.*

(Gen. 41:28-30)

These are only a few examples from the book of Genesis.
Indeed, I could fill many pages by scanning through the
whole Bible.

The point is this: God is not an Immovable Force out of
whom only nice things continually flow. God declared:

*"I am the Lord, and there is no other,
The One forming light and creating darkness,
Causing well-being and creating calamity;
I am the Lord who does all these."*

(Is. 45:6-7)

This understanding is difficult to embrace for those who
have a sun-like image of God. They may reject the idea
that God could create calamity, saying, "God could not
have created any bad things, because there is nothing
bad in Him." Notice that this statement is founded in the
sun-like image of God; it envisions God's creation flowing from out of His own being as light radiating from the
sun. In reality, God creates out of nothing. The things
He creates do not flow out of Him. He speaks and things
come into existence. Therefore, He can be very different
than what He creates.

Compare this with how a carpenter can build a house,
but he does not resemble nor have the same nature as the
house. This is even more true with God. He can create
out of nothing, anything He wants, anytime He wants.

For several years I was involved with a branch of

217

Christianity whose theology simplified everything into good and evil. They often spoke of how good flows out of God and evil flows out of Satan. They defined good as life, health, prosperity, and other natural blessings. They defined evil as death, sickness, poverty and other natural difficulties. I listened to and embraced their theology for some time, but I kept coming across Bible verses which talk about God doing things which did not fit into their category of "good." Eventually I had to change my theology to fit what I was reading in Scripture. From my study, I have concluded that life is not as simplistic as they were teaching me. They had imposed both their understanding of God and Satan on sun-like images.

Scripture makes it clear: God creates light and darkness; He can cause well-being and create calamity (Is. 45:6-7; see also Is. 54:16).

I am not suggesting that God is responsible for all the pain and suffering in the world. I maintain that the vast majority of suffering results from the presence of evil in the world, the activity of demons, the consequences of humanity's sin, and chance occurrences. However, biblical revelation shows that in some situations, God can and does inflict suffering, pain, and even death.

Finally, I want to put this in perspective by reassuring everyone that we can have faith that God will answer prayers and work on our behalf. However, our faith should be based on knowing God as a good Father rather than thinking of Him as a good Force emanating goodness as the sun emanates light.

Chapter 45
Why Do Babies Die?

People live with many unanswered questions. Most can live their lives successfully, ignoring the inner turmoil, yet when confronted with serious pain, injustice, death, or suffering, they cannot reconcile it with their belief that God is good. Much of the unresolved conflicts result from the Classical View of God which has overshadowed the historic Church. Questions get resolved when Christians renew their minds to the revelation of God provided in the Bible.

Let's attempt to resolve this issue of pain and suffering, first applying the Classical View of God and then the Biblical View. As an example, we will use one of the most difficult trials one can face—the death of a baby.

If we hold to the Classical View, then we have only one answer to offer: God wills it. We may offer other "intermediary answers," such as God is teaching people something. Or Satan caused it. Or people's sin is responsible. However, according to the Classical philosophical way of thinking, these things are merely intermediaries standing between us and the timeless, **sovereign** God who ultimately allows, predestines, and causes all things. According to the Classical View of God, He is ultimately responsible.

A mother whose baby dies must grapple with this. If she believes that God is in control, she is left with one question: Why did a loving and good God take her innocent child?

If we have a Biblical View, there are many possible

answers. The death of the baby may have been the result of:

- an accidental fall,
- improper nutrition or care,
- suffocation or poisoning,
- Sudden Infant Death Syndrome,
- the random selection of genes which caused a genetic disorder,
- the result of an infection, virus, or disease,
- a medical problem which we do not understand,
- the activity of Satan or his demons,
- the consequence of a parent's sin,
- God's actions.

Any combination of the above explanations may be possible, along with an unlimited number of other explanations.

I hesitate in including the last one, because I do not want people to credit God with the killing of children. Obviously, we believe that God is good, and I would never want to tell a mother that God killed her baby. However, if we are going to be true to the biblical revelation, then we must include this as one possibility. After David committed adultery with Bathsheba, *"the Lord struck the child"* and *"the child died"* (II Sam. 12:15-18).

Though I admit that God can kill a child, I reject the Classical View which must hold to the idea that every child which dies was ultimately willed by God to die.

If a mother asks why her baby died, the most relevant biblical answer would be that we live in a world where tragedies happen. Things are out of control. We have not yet learned how to manage effectively all disease, nutrition, genetic, and medical problems. Bad things happen. That is why the baby died.

Still, we do not need to leave the bereaved without hope. After King David's baby died, he stated that he cannot bring the child back to life, but someday he would go to be with the child (II Sam. 12:23). Indeed, we have hope to spend time with our loved ones in the next life.

We also have hope in this present life for good to come forth from tragedies. The Apostle Paul wrote:

> *And we know that God causes all things to work together for good to those who love God, to those who are called according to His purpose.*
> (Rom. 8:28)

It does not matter how terrible or tragic things are, God turns things around as a person loves Him and brings his or her life into alignment with His will.

King David lost his first child with Bathsheba as a consequence of his own sin, yet David brought his life back into alignment with the plan of God and a second child was born. This son, Solomon, became the wisest person on Earth, bringing peace to the nation of Israel.

If a person does not bring his or her life into alignment with the plan of God, there is no guarantee that things will work out for his or her good. Tragic things can have tragic results. On the other hand, for those who love God, He will turn tragic events into works of beauty, grace, and glory.

Conclusion

If the leaders in the Bible walked into one of our modern Western churches, they would be bewildered. If they heard a Classical preacher speak of the immutable, impassible, **sovereign** God, they would be deeply troubled.

If Adam heard a modern Christian say that the Garden of Eden was created perfectly peaceful, orderly, and non-harmful, he would wonder which garden that was and why he had to work six days each week tending and keeping his garden.

If Enoch heard a Classical theologian talk about how God is wholly other, incomprehensible, and unlike us in all ways, he would have a long talk with God about that.

If Noah was told that God never takes risks, he would wonder why millions drowned outside the walls of his boat.

If Abraham heard that God will not take counsel from a man, he would explain the true meaning of covenant and tell of his God who allowed him to barter concerning the destruction of Sodom and Gomorrah.

If Moses heard about an impassible god, he would immediately know that that god is not the same God with whom he reasoned so as not destroy to the Hebrew people.

If the Hebrews believed that God is omniscient, they would wonder about the real reason they had to wander in the wilderness for 40 years, since God must have been lying when He said that He was testing them to see what was in their heart.

If Joshua became convinced by a modern theologian that God experiences no emotional changes, he would have to repent for having Achan killed, even though Achan's death caused the Lord to turn *"from the fierceness of His anger"* (Josh. 7:26).

If the writer of the book of Joshua was a Classical theologian, he never would have said that the day the sun stood still was the day *"when the Lord listened to the voice of a man"* (Josh. 10:14).

If Samuel heard that God only answers prayers which match His will, he would wonder why God had him install Saul as king and then later regretted His decision.

If Saul was told by a modern seminary professor that God can never change in the sense of withdrawing his love, he would refute this, saying through tear-filled eyes that God will not always strive with man.

If David was told that God favors all people equally, he would smile but keep his comments to himself.

If Elijah had heard a Reformed preacher say that God is so big that He does not really respond to our prayers, he would never have prayed for the dead son of a widow and the Bible would never have reported that: *"The Lord heard the voice of Elijah, and the life of the child returned to him and he revived"* (I Kings 17:22).

If Hezekiah was told that God never changes His mind, he would call for Isaiah and ask what God actually said to him concerning the lengthening of his life.

If Mordecai held to the Classical View of God, he never would have told Queen Esther that if she failed to speak on behalf of the Jews, God would just use someone else to deliver the people.

If the book of Job had been written by a Classical

theologian, the book would have never been completed, because the author would still be wrestling with the question, "If God is in control, why is there suffering in the world?"

If the Psalm-writer believed in the unconditional love of God flooding over all of humanity like the sun bathes the earth, he never would have written,

> *The Lord tests the righteous and the wicked,*
> *And the one who loves violence His soul hates.*
> (Ps. 11:5)

If Jeremiah had been a Classical theologian, he would have asked God to speak to him straight instead of using so many figures of speech.

If Daniel held to the Classical View of prayer and prophecy, he would not have spent 21 days fasting and praying for God to fulfill His earlier promise to release the Jews from captivity.

If Jonah believed that God never changes His mind, he would have died under that tree still waiting for God to torch the people of Nineveh.

If Hosea thought that God fills all of time, and therefore, He can never change, he would not have married a harlot as a prophetic act to declare that God had turned against Israel.

If John the Baptist had believed that God is equally pleased with all people, he would not have been so impressed by the voice which came out of heaven over Jesus: *"You are My beloved Son, in You I am well-pleased"* (Mark 1:11).

If Peter believed that the time of our Lord's return

was predestined, he never would have put false hope before his readers by saying that they could hasten the coming of the Lord.

If Paul were told that God is **sovereign** in the sense that He causes all things, he would adamantly declare that it was not God who caused him to foolishly kill Christians, but it was God who sovereignly stopped him.

If John was told that God's love is like the sun evenly bathing all people, he would recall the undivided attention he received from Jesus and the warmth he sensed in those moments.

If God took His anger out on Jesus, then He is not very merciful or forgiving.

If God is impassable, the Holy Spirit could never be grieved.

If Jesus walked into a modern church, He would tell us that we should learn to call God, "Father."

Recommended Reading

Boyd, Gregory. *God of the Possible.* (Grand Rapids, MI: Baker Books, 2000).

Boyd, Gregory and Eddy, Paul. *Across the Spectrum.* (Grand Rapids, MI: Baker Academic, 2002).

Eberle, Harold. *Christianity Unshackled.* (Yakima, WA: Worldcast Publishing, 2009).

Pinnock, Clark, et al., *The Openness of God: A Biblical Challenge to the Traditional Understanding of God.* (Downers Grove, IL: InterVarsity Press, 1994).

Sanders, John. *The God Who Risks.* (Downers Grove, IL: InterVarsity Press, 1998).

One ramification of Open theism is the individual taking personal responsibility to cooperate with God to form the future. This includes the formation of society—impacting government, business, education, the arts, communication, entertainment, and all other areas of life. Realizing that God is willing to work with humanity to mold this world, leads and inspires Christians to confidently engage in the affairs of this world to shape it for God's glory.

An excellent book discussing this further is *Releasing Kings for Ministry in the Marketplace,* co-authored by John Garfield and Harold Eberle. You will also want to view a supporting web site (www.Releasing-Kings.com.) where articles are posted and Christians are challenged to accept their God-given callings in the marketplace.

Other Books by Harold R. Eberle

The Complete Wineskin
(Fourth edition)

The Body of Christ is in a reformation. God is pouring out His Holy Spirit and our wineskins must be changed to handle the new wine. Will the Church come together in unity? How does the anointing of God work and what is your role? What is the 5-fold ministry? How are apostles, prophets, evangelists, pastors, and teachers going to rise up and work together? Where do small group meetings fit in? This book puts into words what you have been sensing in your spirit. (Eberle's best seller, translated into many languages, distributed worldwide.)

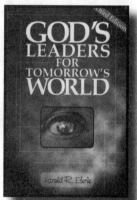

God's Leaders for Tomorrow's World
(Revised/expanded edition)

You sense the call to leadership, but questions persist: "Does God want me to rise up? Do I truly know where to lead? Is this pride? How can I influence people?" Through an understanding of leadership dynamics, learn how to develop godly charisma. Confusion will melt into order when you see the God-ordained lines of authority. Fear of leadership will change to confidence as you learn to handle power struggles. It is time to move into your "metron," that is, your God-given sphere of authority.

Christianity Unshackled
Christianity Separated from the Western Worldview

Most Christians in the Western world have no idea how profoundly their beliefs have been influenced by their culture. After untangling the Western traditions of the last 2,000 years of Church history, Harold R. Eberle offers a Christian worldview that is clear, concise, and liberating. This will leave you shouting in victory! This book is now available as a downloadable book from the web site of Worldcast Publishing. However, it will soon be available in hard copy.

Releasing Kings into the Marketplace for Ministry

Co-authored by
John Garfield and Harold R. Eberle

"Kings" is what we call Christian leaders who have embraced the call of God upon their life to work in the marketplace and from that position transform society. This book explains how marketplace ministry will operate in concert with local churches and pastors. It provides a Scriptural basis for the expansion of the Kingdom of God into all areas of society. It paints a picture of Kings who are naturally competitive, creative, and decisive—who are being used to fulfill the Great Commission.

Destined to Reign,
Seven Keys to Your Marketplace Ministry

This is a sequel to the book described above. Written by John Garfield, it is aimed to bless the nations by releasing an army of kings, having a mission to change cultures with the Gospel of life more abundantly . . . impart the message, make the money, do the mission, and make more disciples that will make a difference.

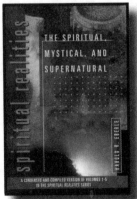

The Spiritual, Mystical, and Supernatural

The first five volumes of Harold R. Eberle's series of books entitled, *Spiritual Realities,* have been condensed into this one volume, 372 pages in length. Topics are addressed such as how the spiritual and natural worlds are related, angelic and demonic manifestations, signs and wonders, miracles and healing, the anointing, good versus evil spiritual practices, how people are created by God to access the spiritual realm, how the spirits of people interact, how people sense things in the spirit realm, and much more.

230

Victorious Eschatology

A Partial Preterist View
Co-authored by
Harold R. Eberle and Martin Trench

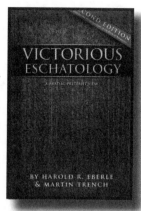

Here it is—a biblically-based, optimistic view of the future. Along with a historical perspective, this book offers a clear understanding of Matthew 24, the book of Revelation, and other key passages about the events to precede the return of Jesus Christ. Satan is not going to take over this world. Jesus Christ is Lord and He will reign until every enemy is put under His feet!

Jesus Came Out of the Tomb... So Can You!

A Brief Explanation of Resurrection-based Christianity

Forgiveness of sins is at the cross. Power over sin is in the resurrection and ascension. Unfortunately, too many Christians have only benefited from the death of Jesus and not His life. If God raised Jesus from the tomb in power and glory, then we can experience that resurrection power. If God raised Jesus into heaven, and us with Him, then we can live in His victory!